Walking Camino de

Discovering Camino's Pilgrim's Route, Camino's Waymarking system, Etiquette and Traditions.

Jay. C Walker, 2024

All rights reserved. No part of this publication may be reproduced, distributed, or transmitted in any form or by any means, including photocopying, recording, or other electronic or mechanical methods, without the prior written permission of the publisher, except in the case of brief quotations embodied in critical reviews and certain other noncommercial uses permitted by copyright law.

Copyright ©Jay. C Walker, 2024

Table of Content

Introduction

About the Author
About the Camino Pilgrim's Route
Why Embark on the Camino Journey
What to Expect from This Guide

Chapter 1: Planning your Pilgrimage

Choosing the Right Route for You
Deciding When to Go
Budgeting and Financial Considerations
Packing Essentials: What to Bring on the Camino
Preparing Physically and Mentally for the Journey

Chapter 2: The Routes

Overview of the Different Camino Routes
Detailed Description of Each Route:
The Camino Francés
The Camino del Norte
The Camino Portugués
The Camino Primitivo
The Camino Inglés
The Via de la Plata

The Camino Finisterre and Muxía
Comparing Routes: Difficulty, Scenery, and Highlights

Chapter 3: Accommodation and Services

Types of Accommodation Along the Camino
Albergues: Pilgrim Hostels Hotels, Guesthouses, and Other Lodging Options
Where to Eat: Restaurants, Cafés, and Pilgrim Menus
Finding Groceries and Supplies Along the Way
Medical Services and Pharmacies

Chapter 4: Navigation and Waymarking

Understanding the Camino's Waymarking System
Using Guidebooks, Maps, and GPS Devices
Tips for Staying on Track and Avoiding Common Pitfalls

Chapter 5: Daily Life on the Camino

A Typical Day as a Pilgrim
Camino Etiquette and Traditions
Making Connections: Camino Companions and Community
Dealing with Challenges and Overcoming Obstacles

Chapter 6: Camino Culture and History

The Historical Significance of the Camino de Santiago
Religious and Spiritual Aspects of the Pilgrimage
Cultural Highlights Along the Way
Stories and Legends of the Camino

Chapter 7: After the Camino

Reflections on Completing the Pilgrimage
Bringing the Camino Spirit Home
Continuing Your Journey: Future Pilgrimages and Camino Resources

Appendice

Useful Resources and Websites
Packing Checklist
Sample Itineraries for Different Routes
Maps

Introduction

About the Author

Jay.C Walker is a seasoned traveler, adventurer, and storyteller with a passion for exploring diverse cultures and landscapes around the world. Born and raised in a small town in the Midwest, Jay developed an early fascination with the unknown, fueled by his voracious appetite for reading and learning about distant lands.

As a young adult, Jay embarked on his first solo journey abroad, igniting a lifelong love affair with travel. Over the years, he has crisscrossed the globe, from the bustling streets of Tokyo to the remote villages of the Andes, seeking out authentic experiences and forging meaningful connections with people from all walks of life.

Jay's wanderlust has taken him on countless adventures, from trekking through dense rainforests in Borneo to summiting snow-capped peaks in the Himalayas. Along the way, he has encountered myriad challenges and triumphs, each serving to deepen his understanding of the world and his place within it.

A firm believer in the transformative power of travel, Jay has made it his mission to inspire others to step out of their comfort zones and embark on their own journeys of discovery. Through his writing, speaking engagements, and social media presence, he shares practical advice, insightful observations, and captivating stories from his travels, encouraging readers and listeners to embrace curiosity, embrace diversity, and embrace the unknown.

In addition to his passion for travel, Jay is also an avid photographer, capturing the beauty and complexity of the world through his lens. His photographs have been featured in numerous publications and exhibitions, earning praise for their ability to evoke emotion and spark imagination.

When he's not on the road, Jay can be found at home in his cozy apartment, surrounded by stacks of travel books and maps, dreaming up his next adventure. He is a firm believer in the power of community and actively participates in online forums and meetups, connecting with fellow travelers and sharing tips and insights gleaned from his experiences.

Jay holds a degree in Cultural Anthropology from a prestigious university, where he specialized in the study of indigenous cultures and sustainable tourism. His academic background informs his approach to travel, emphasizing respect for local customs and traditions, and a commitment to responsible and ethical exploration.

In his spare time, Jay enjoys hiking, meditation, and experimenting with new recipes in the kitchen. He is a firm believer in the importance of self-care and personal growth, and strives to maintain a healthy balance between his adventurous pursuits and his inner journey.

With a wealth of experience and a deep love for the world and its people, Jay.C Walker continues to inspire and empower others to embrace the spirit of adventure and embark on their own transformative journeys, one step at a time. Whether traversing remote mountain trails or navigating bustling city streets, he remains steadfast in his belief that the greatest adventures are yet to come.

About the Camino Pilgrim's Route

The Camino Pilgrim's Route, also known as the Camino de Santiago, is a network of ancient pilgrimage routes leading to the shrine of the apostle Saint James the Great in the Cathedral of Santiago de Compostela in Galicia, northwest Spain. This historic pilgrimage has been traversed by millions of pilgrims over the centuries, drawing people from all walks of life and from every corner of the globe.

History and Origins

The origins of the Camino de Santiago can be traced back to the early Middle Ages when the remains of Saint James were discovered in the ninth century. Legend has it that after James was martyred in Jerusalem, his disciples transported his body by sea to the Iberian Peninsula, where he was buried in what is now Santiago de Compostela. His tomb soon became a site of veneration, attracting pilgrims from across Europe and beyond.

Routes

The Camino Pilgrim's Route comprises several main routes, each with its own unique history, landscape, and cultural significance. The most popular route is the Camino Francés, which stretches nearly 800 kilometers from the French border town of Saint-Jean-Pied-de-Port to Santiago de Compostela. Other notable routes include the Camino del Norte along the northern coast of Spain, the Camino Portugués from Portugal, the Camino Primitivo from Oviedo, and the Via de la Plata from Seville.

Spirituality and Pilgrimage
While the Camino de Santiago has deep roots in Christian tradition, it is also embraced by people of all faiths and backgrounds as a journey of self-discovery, reflection, and spiritual growth. Pilgrims walk the Camino for a variety of reasons – some seek solace or healing, others embark on a quest for adventure or personal challenge, and many simply feel drawn to the mystical allure of the ancient pilgrimage route.

Cultural Highlights
Along the Camino, pilgrims encounter a rich tapestry of cultural and historical landmarks, including medieval villages, Romanesque churches, and UNESCO World Heritage sites. The route passes through diverse landscapes, from lush green valleys and rolling hills to rugged mountains and coastal cliffs, offering breathtaking scenery at every turn. Along the way, pilgrims have the opportunity to immerse themselves in local traditions, sample regional cuisine, and connect with fellow travelers from around the world.

Community and Camino Spirit
One of the most cherished aspects of the Camino Pilgrim's Route is the sense of camaraderie and community that develops among pilgrims along the way. Strangers become friends as they share meals, stories, and experiences, offering support and encouragement to one another through the ups and downs of the journey. The spirit of the Camino, known as "compostela," is characterized by kindness, generosity, and a

shared sense of purpose, transcending cultural and linguistic barriers to unite pilgrims in a common bond of humanity.

Modern-Day Revival

In recent decades, the Camino de Santiago has experienced a resurgence in popularity, attracting pilgrims from all walks of life and from every corner of the globe. Modern amenities such as albergues (pilgrim hostels), waymarking signs, and guidebooks make the journey more accessible than ever before, while maintaining the timeless allure and spiritual significance of this ancient pilgrimage route.

The Camino Pilgrim's Route is more than just a long walk – it is a journey of the soul, a rite of passage, and a testament to the enduring power of human connection and spiritual exploration. Whether undertaken for religious devotion, personal growth, or simply the love of adventure, the Camino offers pilgrims a transformative experience that lingers long after the journey is complete, inspiring them to live with greater purpose, compassion, and gratitude.

Why Embark on the Camino Journey

The decision to embark on the Camino journey is a deeply personal one, influenced by a myriad of factors ranging from spiritual seeking to physical challenge, cultural exploration to personal growth. Below, we explore some of the most compelling reasons why individuals from all walks of life choose to undertake this ancient pilgrimage:

Spiritual Quest
For many pilgrims, the Camino represents a profound spiritual journey, a quest for meaning, connection, and transcendence. Rooted in Christian tradition, the pilgrimage to the shrine of Saint James offers a sacred space for reflection, prayer, and introspection. Whether seeking answers to life's big questions, grappling with grief or loss, or simply yearning for a deeper connection to the divine, the Camino provides a sacred pathway for spiritual seekers to commune with the divine and find solace in the rhythm of their footsteps.

Personal Growth
The Camino journey is a crucible for personal growth and transformation, challenging pilgrims to push beyond their comfort zones, confront their fears, and discover their inner strength. Walking hundreds of kilometers across rugged terrain requires resilience, determination, and perseverance, qualities that are cultivated through the trials and tribulations of the pilgrimage. Along the way, pilgrims are tested physically, mentally, and emotionally, emerging stronger,

wiser, and more self-aware as they navigate the ups and downs of the journey.

Cultural Exploration

The Camino is more than just a religious pilgrimage – it is a cultural odyssey through the heart of Spain, encompassing diverse landscapes, traditions, and heritage. From medieval villages and Romanesque churches to bustling cities and rural hamlets, the Camino route offers pilgrims a rich tapestry of cultural and historical landmarks to explore. Along the way, pilgrims have the opportunity to immerse themselves in local customs, sample regional cuisine, and forge connections with people from all walks of life, gaining a deeper appreciation for the diversity and complexity of the human experience.

Physical Challenge

Walking the Camino is no small feat – it is a physical challenge that demands endurance, stamina, and resilience. From the steep climbs of the Pyrenees to the endless stretches of flat terrain, pilgrims must navigate a variety of landscapes and weather conditions, testing their physical limits every step of the way. Yet, it is precisely through this physical exertion that many pilgrims find a sense of empowerment and accomplishment, pushing themselves beyond perceived limitations and discovering the incredible capabilities of the human body.

Camino Community

One of the most cherished aspects of the Camino journey is the sense of camaraderie and community that develops among pilgrims along the way. Strangers become friends as they share meals, stories, and experiences, offering support and encouragement to one another through the ups and downs of the journey. The spirit of the Camino, known as "compostela," is characterized by kindness, generosity, and a shared sense of purpose, transcending cultural and linguistic barriers to unite pilgrims in a common bond of humanity.

Whether undertaken for spiritual seeking, personal growth, cultural exploration, physical challenge, or community connection, the Camino journey offers pilgrims a transformative experience that lingers long after the journey is complete. It is a pilgrimage of the heart, a pilgrimage of the soul, inviting travelers to embark on a sacred quest for meaning, purpose, and connection in an ever-changing world.

What to Expect from This Guide

Welcome to your comprehensive guide to the Camino Pilgrim's Route. Whether you're a seasoned traveler or embarking on your first pilgrimage, this guide is designed to provide you with all the information, resources, and inspiration you need to make the most of your Camino journey. Here's what you can expect to find within these pages:

In-depth Route Information

Gain a comprehensive understanding of the various Camino routes, including the Camino Francés, Camino del Norte, Camino Portugués, Camino Primitivo, Via de la Plata, and more. Each route is detailed with information on distances, terrain, landmarks, and highlights, allowing you to choose the route that best suits your preferences and abilities.

Practical Planning Tips

Receive expert advice on planning and preparing for your pilgrimage, covering topics such as when to go, what to pack, how to train, and budgeting for your trip. Learn how to obtain a pilgrim credential, make accommodation reservations, and navigate logistical challenges along the way, ensuring a smooth and enjoyable journey from start to finish.

Cultural and Historical Insights

Immerse yourself in the rich history, culture, and heritage of the Camino, with detailed insights into the religious significance, architectural marvels, and cultural traditions encountered along the route. Discover the stories behind ancient churches, medieval villages, and sacred sites, gaining a deeper appreciation for the spiritual and cultural tapestry of the Camino.

Accommodation and Services Guide

Navigate the plethora of accommodation options available to pilgrims, from pilgrim hostels and albergues to hotels, guesthouses, and alternative lodging. Find practical information on where to eat, rest, and replenish supplies along the way, ensuring you have everything you need for a comfortable and fulfilling pilgrimage experience.

Navigation and Waymarking Tips

Learn how to navigate the Camino route with confidence, with guidance on understanding the waymarking system, using guidebooks, maps, and GPS devices, and staying on course even in the most remote and challenging terrain. Gain insider tips and tricks for avoiding common navigation pitfalls and making the most of your time on the trail.

Daily Life on the Camino

Discover what a typical day on the Camino looks like, from sunrise to sunset, with insights into daily routines, walking pace, rest breaks, and cultural customs. Learn about Camino etiquette and traditions, connect with fellow pilgrims, and embrace the spirit of camaraderie and community that defines the Camino experience.

Reflections and Resources

Wrap up your Camino journey with reflections on your pilgrimage experience, tips for bringing the Camino spirit home, and resources for further exploration and inspiration. Whether you're planning future pilgrimages or simply seeking to integrate the lessons learned on the Camino into your everyday life, this guide will empower you to continue your journey long after the trail has ended.

With comprehensive route information, practical planning tips, cultural insights, and resources for further exploration, this guide is your essential companion for embarking on the Camino Pilgrim's Route. Whether you're seeking spiritual renewal, personal growth, cultural immersion, or simply the adventure of a lifetime, let this guide be your roadmap to a transformative pilgrimage experience you'll never forget.

Chapter 1: Planning your Pilgrimage

Planning your pilgrimage on the Camino involves careful consideration of various factors to ensure a smooth and fulfilling journey. Begin by selecting the Camino route that best suits your preferences, abilities, and timeframe, taking into account factors such as weather conditions, crowd levels, and cultural attractions along the route. Research accommodation options, transportation logistics, and cultural events along the way, and create a detailed itinerary that outlines your daily walking distances, rest stops, and points of interest. Pack light but thoughtfully, considering essential gear, clothing, and supplies to meet your needs on the trail. Prioritize physical and mental preparation, including training, injury prevention, and resilience-building techniques, to ensure you're ready to embrace the challenges and rewards of the pilgrimage experience. Lastly, maintain flexibility and an open mind as you embark on your journey, allowing for serendipitous encounters, unexpected detours, and meaningful moments along the way.

Choosing the Right Route for You

Embarking on the Camino Pilgrim's Route is a deeply personal journey, and selecting the right route is essential to ensuring a fulfilling and rewarding pilgrimage experience. With a variety of routes to choose from, each offering its own unique landscapes, challenges, and cultural attractions, it's important to consider your interests, abilities, and preferences when making your decision. Here's a detailed guide to help you choose the route that best suits you:

Consider Your Physical Fitness and Abilities

Before selecting a route, honestly assess your physical fitness level and hiking experience. Some routes, such as the Camino Francés, involve long daily distances and challenging terrain, while others, like the Camino Portugués, offer a more relaxed pace and gentler gradients. Choose a route that matches your fitness level and hiking preferences to ensure an enjoyable and manageable journey.

Determine Your Timeframe

Consider how much time you have available for your pilgrimage and choose a route that aligns with your timeframe. Longer routes, such as the Camino Francés or the Camino del Norte, may require several weeks to complete, while shorter routes, like the Camino Inglés or the Camino Finisterre, can be completed in as little as a week. Be realistic about the amount of time you can commit to your pilgrimage and choose a route accordingly.

Explore Your Interests and Preferences

Think about what aspects of the Camino experience are most important to you and choose a route that aligns with your interests and preferences. If you're drawn to stunning coastal scenery, consider the Camino del Norte or the Camino Portugués along the Atlantic coast. If you're interested in exploring historic towns and cultural landmarks, the Camino Francés offers a wealth of architectural treasures and UNESCO World Heritage sites.

Reflect on Your Spiritual Goals

For many pilgrims, the Camino is a deeply spiritual journey, offering an opportunity for reflection, prayer, and inner transformation. Consider your spiritual goals and choose a route that resonates with your beliefs and values. Some routes, like the Camino Francés or the Camino Portugués, have strong religious significance and are popular among pilgrims seeking a traditional pilgrimage experience. Others, like the Camino Primitivo or the Via de la Plata, offer a more solitary and contemplative journey through remote landscapes and ancient forests.

Research Route Highlights and Attractions

Take the time to research the highlights and attractions along each route to get a sense of what you can expect to encounter during your pilgrimage. Consider whether you're interested in visiting historic cathedrals, sampling regional cuisine, or exploring natural wonders, and choose a route that offers the experiences and attractions that resonate with you.

Seek Advice from Experienced Pilgrims

Reach out to experienced pilgrims, either online or in person, to gather insights and recommendations on choosing a route. Fellow pilgrims can offer valuable advice based on their own experiences, helping you make an informed decision that aligns with your goals and preferences.

Deciding When to Go

Embarking on the Camino Pilgrimage is a significant journey that requires careful consideration of when to go. The timing of your pilgrimage can greatly impact your experience, influencing factors such as weather conditions, crowd levels, accommodation availability, and cultural events along the route. In this comprehensive guide, we will explore the various factors to consider when deciding when to go on the Camino, empowering you to choose the optimal time for your pilgrimage.

Weather Conditions

One of the most important factors to consider when deciding when to go on the Camino is the weather. The climate along the Camino routes varies depending on the time of year and the specific route you choose. Generally, the spring (April to June) and fall (September to October) months are considered the best times to walk the Camino, as the weather is typically mild and pleasant, with fewer extremes in temperature and less rainfall. Summer (July to August) can be hot and crowded, especially in popular sections of the route, while winter (November to March) can be cold, wet, and challenging, particularly in higher elevations and mountainous regions. Consider your tolerance for different weather conditions and choose a time of year that aligns with your preferences and comfort level.

Crowds and Accommodation Availability

Another important consideration when deciding when to go on the Camino is the level of crowds and availability of accommodation along the route. The Camino has experienced a surge in popularity in recent years, especially during the peak summer months, when the trails can become crowded with pilgrims from around the world. This can lead to competition for accommodation, particularly in popular towns and villages along the route. If you prefer a quieter, more solitary pilgrimage experience, consider walking during the shoulder seasons of spring or fall, when the crowds are smaller and accommodation is more readily available. Alternatively, if you thrive on the camaraderie and social atmosphere of the Camino, summer may be the ideal time for you to go.

Cultural Events and Festivals

The Camino routes pass through numerous towns and villages that host cultural events, festivals, and religious celebrations throughout the year. Participating in these events can add a unique and memorable dimension to your pilgrimage experience, offering insight into local traditions and customs. Research the calendar of events along your chosen route and consider timing your pilgrimage to coincide with festivals such as Semana Santa (Holy Week) in Spain, the Feast of Saint James in July, or the grape harvest festivals in the wine-growing regions of La Rioja and Galicia. These events provide opportunities for cultural immersion, community engagement, and spiritual enrichment, enhancing your overall Camino experience.

Personal Commitments and Obligations

Before deciding when to go on the Camino, consider any personal commitments or obligations that may impact your travel plans. Evaluate factors such as work schedules, family responsibilities, and financial constraints, and choose a time of year that allows you to dedicate sufficient time and attention to your pilgrimage without undue stress or pressure. Keep in mind that walking the Camino requires a significant time investment, ranging from several weeks to several months depending on the route and pace of travel, so be sure to plan accordingly and make arrangements to accommodate your absence from home.

Physical and Mental Preparation

Finally, consider your own physical and mental readiness for the pilgrimage when deciding when to go on the Camino. Walking the Camino requires a certain level of physical fitness, stamina, and mental resilience to cope with the physical demands of long days of walking, as well as the psychological challenges of being away from home and navigating unfamiliar terrain. Take the time to prepare your body and mind for the journey ahead, engaging in regular exercise, hiking, and mental relaxation techniques to build strength, endurance, and resilience. Choose a time of year that allows you to adequately prepare for the pilgrimage and embark on your journey feeling confident, capable, and ready for the adventure ahead.

Budgeting and Financial Considerations

Embarking on the Camino Pilgrimage is a transformative journey that requires careful planning and budgeting to ensure a rewarding and fulfilling experience. Whether you're walking the Camino Francés, Camino del Norte, Camino Portugués, or any other route, it's important to consider your financial resources and expenses to make the most of your pilgrimage. In this comprehensive guide, we will explore various budgeting strategies and financial considerations to help you plan and prepare for your Camino journey.

Establishing Your Budget

The first step in planning your Camino pilgrimage is to establish a realistic budget based on your financial resources, preferences, and priorities. Consider factors such as transportation costs to and from the Camino, daily expenses while on the pilgrimage (such as accommodation, meals, and incidentals), as well as any additional expenses for gear, equipment, travel insurance, and emergency funds. Take the time to carefully assess your income, savings, and available resources, and determine how much you can comfortably afford to spend on your pilgrimage without jeopardizing your financial security.

Researching Costs Along the Route

Once you've established your budget, research the typical costs associated with walking the Camino along your chosen route. Costs can vary depending on factors such as the time of year, the popularity of the route, and your personal preferences for accommodation and dining. Research the average cost of accommodation in albergues (pilgrim hostels), hotels, and guesthouses along the route, as well as the cost of meals, snacks, and drinks at restaurants, cafés, and grocery stores. Additionally, consider any additional expenses for transportation, sightseeing, souvenirs, and other discretionary spending.

Identifying Ways to Save Money

While walking the Camino can be a relatively affordable travel option compared to other forms of tourism, there are still opportunities to save money and stretch your budget further. Consider staying in albergues or municipal pilgrim hostels, which are often the most affordable accommodation options along the route. Take advantage of pilgrim menus and communal meals offered at local restaurants and cafés, which typically provide hearty, budget-friendly fare for pilgrims. Be mindful of unnecessary expenses and avoid overspending on non-essential items or experiences that don't align with your priorities and goals for the pilgrimage.

Planning for Unexpected Expenses

No matter how carefully you budget and plan, it's important to anticipate and prepare for unexpected expenses that may arise during your Camino pilgrimage. Set aside a contingency fund or emergency savings to cover unforeseen costs such as medical expenses, transportation disruptions, gear replacements, or other emergencies. Consider purchasing travel insurance to protect yourself financially in case of illness, injury, or other unexpected events that may impact your pilgrimage. By planning ahead and being proactive about budgeting for potential contingencies, you can minimize stress and uncertainty and focus on enjoying your pilgrimage experience to the fullest.

Tracking Your Expenses

Once you're on the Camino, it's important to track your expenses and stay within your budget to avoid overspending and running out of funds before reaching your destination. Keep a detailed record of your daily expenses, including accommodation, meals, transportation, and any other costs incurred along the way. Use a budgeting app, spreadsheet, or notebook to track your spending and monitor your progress towards your budgetary goals. Regularly review your expenses and adjust your spending as needed to stay on track and ensure that you have enough funds to complete your pilgrimage comfortably and safely.

Packing Essentials: What to Bring on the Camino

Embarking on the Camino Pilgrimage requires careful consideration of what to pack to ensure you have everything you need for a comfortable and fulfilling journey. While it's essential to pack light to minimize the weight you carry, it's equally important to bring the right essentials to meet your needs along the way. In this detailed guide, we'll explore the essential items you should pack for your Camino pilgrimage, helping you prepare for the adventure of a lifetime.

Backpack
A well-fitting, lightweight backpack is essential for carrying your belongings while walking the Camino. Choose a backpack with padded shoulder straps, a supportive waist belt, and multiple compartments for organizing your gear. Opt for a size that comfortably accommodates your essentials without being too bulky or heavy.

Clothing
Pack lightweight, moisture-wicking clothing that can be layered for warmth and protection against the elements. Essentials include:

Quick-drying t-shirts and long-sleeved shirts
Breathable, moisture-wicking underwear and socks
Lightweight pants or shorts
Fleece or lightweight jacket for cooler evenings
Waterproof and windproof outer layer

Hat, sunglasses, and sunscreen for sun protection
Comfortable walking shoes or hiking boots with good ankle support
Flip-flops or lightweight sandals for relaxing in the evenings

Gear and Equipment

Bring essential gear and equipment to enhance your comfort and safety on the Camino. Consider packing:

Lightweight, quick-drying towel
Sleeping bag or sleep sack for staying in albergues
Travel-sized toiletries, including soap, shampoo, toothpaste, and sunscreen
Personal hygiene items such as wet wipes, hand sanitizer, and tissues
Small first aid kit with bandages, antiseptic, blister treatment, and pain relievers
Multi-tool or pocket knife for emergencies
Headlamp or flashlight for navigating in low light
Reusable water bottle or hydration system to stay hydrated on the trail
Trekking poles for added stability and support while walking

Electronics and Communication

While you may want to disconnect and immerse yourself in the pilgrimage experience, it's still important to bring essential electronics and communication devices for safety and convenience. Consider packing:

Smartphone with GPS navigation apps, camera, and communication capabilities

Portable charger or power bank to recharge your devices
Lightweight travel adapter and charging cables
Lightweight, waterproof pouch or case to protect your electronics from moisture and dust

Miscellaneous Items

Don't forget to pack a few miscellaneous items to enhance your comfort and convenience on the Camino. Consider bringing:

Lightweight, quick-drying travel towel
Earplugs and eye mask for sleeping in dormitory-style accommodations
Small daypack or waist pack for day trips and excursions
Travel journal and pen for recording your thoughts, reflections, and experiences along the way
Ziplock bags or dry sacks for organizing and protecting your belongings from moisture
Guidebook, map, or smartphone app with information on the Camino route, accommodations, and points of interest

Pilgrim Credential

Lastly, don't forget to obtain a pilgrim credential (credencial del peregrino) before starting your Camino journey. This official document serves as your passport along the route, allowing you to stay in pilgrim accommodations and receive stamps (sellos) at churches, albergues, and other designated locations to verify your pilgrimage. Carry your credential with you at all times and present it when checking into accommodations or receiving services along the route.

Preparing Physically and Mentally for the Journey

Embarking on the Camino Pilgrimage is not only a physical challenge but also a mental and emotional journey that requires careful preparation and readiness. Walking hundreds of kilometers over several weeks or months can take a toll on your body and mind, so it's essential to prepare yourself physically, mentally, and emotionally for the pilgrimage ahead. In this detailed guide, we'll explore the key steps you can take to prepare yourself for the Camino journey, ensuring you're ready to embrace the challenges and rewards that lie ahead.

Physical Preparation

Start Training Early

Begin training for the Camino well in advance to build strength, endurance, and resilience in your body. Incorporate regular walking, hiking, and cardiovascular exercises into your routine to gradually increase your fitness level and prepare your muscles, joints, and cardiovascular system for the demands of long-distance walking.

Gradually Increase Walking Distance

Gradually increase the distance and intensity of your walks over time to simulate the conditions of the Camino. Start with shorter walks and gradually increase the duration and distance each week, incorporating uphill and downhill terrain to prepare for the varied terrain you'll encounter along the route.

Practice Walking with Your Backpack

Get accustomed to walking with a loaded backpack by gradually adding weight to your pack during training walks. Start with a light load and gradually increase the weight over time to simulate the conditions of carrying your belongings on the Camino. Focus on maintaining good posture and walking mechanics to minimize strain and discomfort on your back and shoulders.

Strengthen Your Core and Lower Body

Focus on strengthening your core muscles, legs, and feet to improve stability, balance, and endurance while walking. Incorporate exercises such as squats, lunges, planks, and calf raises into your training routine to target key muscle groups used for walking and hiking.

Practice Self-Care and Injury Prevention

Prioritize self-care and injury prevention to keep your body in optimal condition throughout your training and pilgrimage. Pay attention to any signs of fatigue, discomfort, or pain during training walks and address them promptly with rest, ice, compression, and elevation (RICE) as needed. Listen to your body and adjust your training intensity and duration accordingly to prevent overuse injuries and burnout.

Mental and Emotional Preparation

Set Realistic Expectations

Set realistic expectations for your Camino journey and acknowledge that it will be both physically and mentally challenging at times. Embrace the ups and downs of the pilgrimage experience, knowing that each step brings you closer to your destination and personal goals.

Cultivate Resilience and Mindfulness

Cultivate resilience and mindfulness to cope with the inevitable challenges and uncertainties you'll encounter along the Camino. Practice techniques such as deep breathing, meditation, and visualization to stay grounded, centered, and present in the moment, especially during difficult or stressful situations.

Build Confidence and Self-Efficacy

Build confidence and self-efficacy by setting small, achievable goals for yourself during training and gradually increasing the difficulty and complexity over time. Celebrate your progress and accomplishments along the way, no matter how small, and use them as motivation to keep moving forward on your journey.

Develop Coping Strategies for Challenges

Develop coping strategies and resilience-building techniques to navigate the inevitable challenges and obstacles you'll face on the Camino. Whether it's physical discomfort, inclement weather, navigation difficulties, or interpersonal conflicts, have a toolkit of strategies such as positive self-talk, problem-solving skills, and social support to help you overcome adversity and stay focused on your goals.

Practice Gratitude and Mindfulness

Practice gratitude and mindfulness to cultivate a sense of appreciation and presence throughout your Camino journey.

Take time each day to reflect on the beauty and wonder of the natural world around you, connect with fellow pilgrims, and express gratitude for the opportunity to embark on this transformative pilgrimage experience.

Chapter 2: The Routes

The Camino offers a diverse range of routes, each with its own unique landscapes, cultural attractions, and historical significance. The Camino Francés, the most popular route, traverses the heart of Spain from the Pyrenees to Santiago de Compostela, passing through picturesque villages, rolling countryside, and historic cities such as Pamplona, Burgos, and León. The Camino del Norte hugs the rugged coastline of northern Spain, offering stunning ocean views, lush forests, and charming seaside towns along the way. The Camino Portugués follows ancient pathways from Lisbon or Porto to Santiago, passing through lush vineyards, historic towns, and scenic river valleys. Other routes, such as the Camino Primitivo, Via de la Plata, and Camino Inglés, offer alternative paths through diverse landscapes and cultural regions, providing pilgrims with a wide array of options to explore and experience the beauty and diversity of the Camino pilgrimage.

Choosing the Right Route for You: A Comprehensive Guide to Selecting Your Camino Pilgrimage Path

Embarking on the Camino Pilgrimage is a deeply personal journey, and selecting the right route is crucial to ensuring a fulfilling and rewarding experience. With a multitude of routes to choose from, each offering its own unique landscapes, challenges, and cultural attractions, it's important to carefully consider your preferences, abilities, and goals when making your decision. In this comprehensive guide, we will explore the myriad factors to consider when choosing the right Camino route for you, empowering you to embark on a pilgrimage that resonates with your spirit and enriches your soul.

Understanding the Camino Routes

The Camino de Santiago encompasses a network of pilgrimage routes that crisscross Europe and converge at the tomb of Saint James in Santiago de Compostela, Spain. While the Camino Francés is the most well-known and traveled route, there are numerous alternative paths that offer diverse landscapes, cultural experiences, and spiritual encounters. Each route has its own unique character, challenges, and highlights, ranging from rugged coastlines and mountainous terrain to lush forests and rolling countryside. By understanding the distinct characteristics of each route, you can choose the path that aligns with your interests, preferences, and aspirations for the pilgrimage.

Considering Your Physical Fitness and Abilities

One of the most important factors to consider when choosing a Camino route is your physical fitness level and hiking experience. Some routes, such as the Camino Francés and Camino del Norte, involve long daily distances and challenging terrain, while others, like the Camino Portugués or Camino Primitivo, offer a more relaxed pace and gentler gradients. Assess your fitness level honestly and choose a route that matches your abilities, taking into account factors such as age, health conditions, and previous hiking experience. Remember that walking the Camino is a marathon, not a sprint, and it's essential to choose a route that you can comfortably complete within your physical limitations.

Assessing Your Timeframe and Schedule

Consider how much time you have available for your pilgrimage and choose a route that aligns with your timeframe and schedule. Longer routes, such as the Camino Francés or the Camino del Norte, may require several weeks to complete, while shorter routes, like the Camino Inglés or the Camino Finisterre, can be completed in as little as a week. Be realistic about the amount of time you can commit to your pilgrimage and choose a route accordingly. Keep in mind that walking the Camino is not just about reaching your destination, but also about embracing the journey and savoring the experiences along the way. Allow yourself enough time to walk at a comfortable pace, take rest days as needed, and immerse yourself fully in the pilgrimage experience.

Exploring Your Interests and Preferences

Think about what aspects of the Camino experience are most important to you and choose a route that aligns with your interests and preferences. If you're drawn to stunning coastal scenery, consider the Camino del Norte or the Camino Portugués along the Atlantic coast. If you're interested in exploring historic towns and cultural landmarks, the Camino Francés offers a wealth of architectural treasures and UNESCO World Heritage sites. Consider whether you prefer solitude and contemplation or social interaction and camaraderie, and choose a route that offers the experiences and atmosphere that resonate with you.

Reflecting on Your Spiritual Goals

For many pilgrims, the Camino is a deeply spiritual journey, offering an opportunity for reflection, prayer, and inner transformation. Consider your spiritual goals and choose a route that resonates with your beliefs and values. Some routes, like the Camino Francés or the Camino Portugués, have strong religious significance and are popular among pilgrims seeking a traditional pilgrimage experience. Others, like the Camino Primitivo or the Via de la Plata, offer a more solitary and contemplative journey through remote landscapes and ancient forests. Reflect on the type of spiritual experience you're seeking and choose a route that aligns with your intentions and aspirations for the pilgrimage.

Researching Route Highlights and Attractions

Take the time to research the highlights and attractions along each route to get a sense of what you can expect to encounter during your pilgrimage. Consider whether you're interested in visiting historic cathedrals, sampling regional cuisine, or exploring natural wonders, and choose a route that offers the experiences and attractions that resonate with you. Research the cultural events, festivals, and religious celebrations that take place along the route and consider timing your pilgrimage to coincide with these special events for a more enriching and memorable experience.

Seeking Advice from Experienced Pilgrims

Reach out to experienced pilgrims, either online or in person, to gather insights and recommendations on choosing a route. Fellow pilgrims can offer valuable advice based on their own experiences, helping you make an informed decision that aligns with your goals and preferences. Join online forums, social media groups, or local Camino associations to connect with other pilgrims, ask questions, and share tips and advice. Remember that everyone's Camino journey is unique, and what works for one pilgrim may not necessarily work for another. Trust your instincts and choose the route that feels right for you based on your own interests, abilities, and aspirations for the pilgrimage.

The Camino Francés: A Detailed Exploration of the Historic Pilgrimage Route

The Camino Francés, also known as the French Way, is the most famous and heavily traveled route of the Camino de Santiago pilgrimage network. Stretching approximately 780 kilometers (485 miles) across northern Spain, the Camino Francés begins in the French Pyrenees at the town of Saint-Jean-Pied-de-Port and culminates at the Cathedral of Santiago de Compostela, where the remains of Saint James are believed to be interred. This historic pilgrimage route has been traversed by millions of pilgrims over the centuries, following in the footsteps of medieval pilgrims who sought spiritual renewal, forgiveness of sins, and the blessings of Saint James.

Route Highlights

The Camino Francés traverses a diverse and scenic landscape, passing through picturesque villages, rolling countryside, lush vineyards, and historic cities. Along the route, pilgrims encounter numerous cultural and architectural treasures, including medieval cathedrals, Romanesque churches, and ancient monasteries. Highlights of the Camino Francés include:

The Pyrenees: Pilgrims begin their journey in the French Pyrenees, crossing the rugged mountain range via the Route Napoleon or the Valcarlos route, both of which offer stunning vistas and challenging terrain.

Roncesvalles: The first major stop on the Camino Francés, Roncesvalles is home to the Royal Collegiate Church of Roncesvalles, a historic monastery that has provided hospitality to pilgrims for centuries.

Pamplona: The capital of the Navarre region, Pamplona is famous for its annual Running of the Bulls during the San Fermín festival. Pilgrims can explore the city's medieval old town, fortified walls, and Gothic cathedral.

La Rioja: Known for its world-class wine production, the region of La Rioja is a highlight of the Camino Francés, with vineyard-covered hillsides, charming wine villages, and historic monasteries.

Burgos: This historic city is home to the magnificent Burgos Cathedral, a UNESCO World Heritage site renowned for its Gothic architecture and rich artistic heritage.

León: Another major city along the Camino Francés, León boasts a wealth of historic landmarks, including the stunning Gothic cathedral, the Basilica of San Isidoro, and the Romanesque Convent of San Marcos.

Galicia: The final leg of the Camino Francés takes pilgrims through the lush green landscapes of Galicia, known for its misty forests, rolling hills, and quaint stone villages. Highlights include the Cruz de Ferro, the medieval town of Sarria, and the iconic Monte do Gozo viewpoint overlooking Santiago de Compostela.

Accommodation and Services

The Camino Francés is well-served by a network of pilgrim accommodations, including albergues (hostels), guesthouses, hotels, and private hostels. Pilgrims have the option to stay in communal dormitories with bunk beds or private rooms, depending on their preferences and budget. Along the route, pilgrims also have access to a range of services and amenities, including restaurants, cafes, grocery stores, pharmacies, and medical facilities. The infrastructure along the Camino Francés is well-developed, making it relatively easy for pilgrims to find accommodation, food, and other necessities throughout their journey.

Cultural and Spiritual Significance

The Camino Francés holds deep cultural and spiritual significance for pilgrims of all backgrounds and beliefs. For many, walking the Camino is a transformative journey of self-discovery, reflection, and personal growth. Pilgrims have the opportunity to connect with nature, meet fellow travelers from around the world, and explore the rich history and heritage of the Camino. Along the way, pilgrims are invited to pause, reflect, and contemplate the deeper meaning of their pilgrimage experience, whether it be a quest for spiritual enlightenment, a physical challenge, or a cultural immersion.

The Camino del Norte: A Coastal Journey of Discovery and Beauty

The Camino del Norte, also known as the Northern Way, is a breathtaking pilgrimage route that follows the rugged coastline of northern Spain, offering pilgrims stunning ocean views, lush forests, and charming seaside towns. Stretching approximately 825 kilometers (513 miles) from the Basque Country to Santiago de Compostela, the Camino del Norte is renowned for its natural beauty, cultural diversity, and rich history. In this detailed exploration, we'll delve into the highlights, challenges, and unique characteristics of the Camino del Norte, inviting pilgrims to embark on a transformative journey along this iconic pilgrimage route.

Route Highlights

The Camino del Norte winds its way along the northern coast of Spain, passing through picturesque villages, lush green valleys, and rugged coastal landscapes. Highlights of the route include:

San Sebastián: Pilgrims begin their journey in the vibrant seaside city of San Sebastián, known for its stunning beaches, world-class cuisine, and Basque cultural heritage.

Gipuzkoa Coast: The Camino del Norte hugs the scenic coastline of Gipuzkoa, offering breathtaking views of the Bay of Biscay and the rugged cliffs of the Basque Country.

Bilbao: The largest city in the Basque Country, Bilbao is home to the iconic Guggenheim Museum, a masterpiece of modern architecture and contemporary art.

Cantabrian Coast: As the route continues westward, pilgrims traverse the lush green landscapes of Cantabria, passing through charming fishing villages, rolling hills, and dense forests.

Asturian Coast: Asturias is renowned for its dramatic coastline, rugged mountains, and picturesque fishing ports, including the historic town of Luarca and the seaside resort of Ribadesella.

Oviedo: The capital of Asturias, Oviedo is a UNESCO World Heritage site known for its medieval old town, historic monuments, and rich cultural heritage.

Galician Coast: The final leg of the Camino del Norte takes pilgrims through the lush green landscapes of Galicia, where they encounter misty forests, rolling hills, and quaint stone villages.

Challenges and Considerations

While the Camino del Norte offers unparalleled beauty and cultural richness, it also presents unique challenges and considerations for pilgrims. The route is characterized by steep climbs, rugged terrain, and variable weather conditions, especially along the coastal sections where wind and rain can be common. Pilgrims should be prepared for challenging hiking conditions and be mindful of their physical fitness and stamina. Additionally, the Camino del Norte is less developed in terms of infrastructure compared to other routes, with fewer pilgrim accommodations and services along the way. Pilgrims should plan their journey accordingly, ensuring they have adequate provisions, including water, food, and protective gear.

Cultural and Spiritual Significance

The Camino del Norte holds deep cultural and spiritual significance for pilgrims, offering a unique blend of Basque, Cantabrian, Asturian, and Galician cultures along the way. Pilgrims have the opportunity to immerse themselves in the rich traditions, cuisine, and customs of the regions they pass through, connecting with local communities and fellow travelers from around the world. The Camino del Norte also offers numerous opportunities for spiritual reflection and contemplation, with its stunning natural beauty and tranquil coastal landscapes providing a serene backdrop for personal introspection and spiritual growth.

The Camino Portugués: A Journey Through History, Culture, and Natural Beauty

The Camino Portugués, also known as the Portuguese Way, is a historic pilgrimage route that stretches from Lisbon or Porto to Santiago de Compostela, offering pilgrims a rich tapestry of history, culture, and natural beauty along the way. This detailed exploration will delve into the highlights, challenges, and unique characteristics of the Camino Portugués, inviting pilgrims to embark on a transformative journey through the heart of Portugal and Spain.

Route Highlights

The Camino Portugués offers pilgrims two main starting points: Lisbon, the capital city of Portugal, or Porto, famous for its historic center and port wine production. Highlights of the route include:

Lisbon: Pilgrims beginning their journey in Lisbon are treated to the city's vibrant atmosphere, historic landmarks, and cultural attractions, including the iconic Jerónimos Monastery and Belém Tower.

Porto: Starting in Porto allows pilgrims to explore the city's UNESCO-listed historic center, picturesque riverside neighborhoods, and famous wine cellars along the Douro River.

Coastal and Inland Routes: The Camino Portugués offers two main route options: the Coastal Route, which follows the Atlantic coastline through charming fishing villages and sandy beaches, and the Central Route, which meanders through the picturesque countryside and historic towns of inland Portugal.

Ponte de Lima: This historic town is known for its charming medieval center, Roman bridge, and traditional Portuguese architecture, providing a tranquil and scenic stop along the Camino.

Santiago de Compostela: The final destination of the Camino Portugués is the majestic Cathedral of Santiago de Compostela, where pilgrims gather to pay homage to Saint James and receive their compostela, or certificate of pilgrimage.

Challenges and Considerations

While the Camino Portugués is generally considered to be one of the easier and more accessible routes, it still presents its own set of challenges and considerations for pilgrims. The Coastal Route, in particular, can be subject to rough terrain, inclement weather, and limited infrastructure, requiring careful planning and preparation. Pilgrims should also be mindful of the distance and terrain of each stage, pacing themselves accordingly to avoid overexertion and fatigue. Additionally, pilgrims should be prepared for variable weather conditions, especially during the winter months when rain and cold temperatures are more common.

Cultural and Spiritual Significance

The Camino Portugués holds deep cultural and spiritual significance for pilgrims, offering a unique blend of Portuguese and Galician cultures along the way. Pilgrims have the opportunity to explore historic landmarks, medieval towns, and cultural attractions, connecting with local communities and fellow travelers from around the world. The Camino Portugués also provides numerous opportunities for spiritual reflection and contemplation, with its scenic landscapes and tranquil countryside offering a serene backdrop for personal introspection and spiritual growth.

The Camino Primitivo: A Path of Ancient Origins and Natural Splendor

The Camino Primitivo, often referred to as the Original Way, is one of the oldest pilgrimage routes to Santiago de Compostela, tracing its roots back to the 9th century. This historic trail begins in the town of Oviedo, in the lush green landscapes of Asturias, and winds its way through rugged mountains, verdant valleys, and picturesque villages before reaching the hallowed grounds of Santiago de Compostela. In this detailed exploration, we will delve into the highlights, challenges, and unique characteristics of the Camino Primitivo, inviting pilgrims to embark on a journey of ancient origins and natural splendor.

Route Highlights

The Camino Primitivo offers pilgrims a journey of unparalleled beauty and cultural richness, with highlights including:

Oviedo: Pilgrims begin their journey in the historic city of Oviedo, known for its stunning Gothic cathedral, pre-Romanesque churches, and rich artistic heritage.

Asturian Mountains: The Camino Primitivo traverses the rugged peaks and verdant valleys of the Asturian Mountains, offering breathtaking vistas and challenging terrain.

Hospitales Route: Considered one of the most scenic and challenging sections of the Camino Primitivo, the Hospitales

Route passes through remote mountain landscapes and ancient pilgrim hospitals, providing pilgrims with a true sense of solitude and spiritual reflection.

Lugo: As pilgrims approach Santiago de Compostela, they pass through the historic city of Lugo, known for its well-preserved Roman walls, medieval old town, and UNESCO World Heritage status.

Santiago de Compostela: The final destination of the Camino Primitivo is the majestic Cathedral of Santiago de Compostela, where pilgrims gather to pay homage to Saint James and receive their compostela, or certificate of pilgrimage.

Challenges and Considerations

The Camino Primitivo is renowned for its challenging terrain, with steep ascents and descents, rocky paths, and unpredictable weather conditions. Pilgrims should be prepared for rugged hiking conditions and be mindful of their physical fitness and stamina. Additionally, the Camino Primitivo is less developed in terms of infrastructure compared to other routes, with fewer pilgrim accommodations and services along the way. Pilgrims should plan their journey accordingly, ensuring they have adequate provisions, including water, food, and protective gear.

Cultural and Spiritual Significance

The Camino Primitivo holds deep cultural and spiritual significance for pilgrims, offering a journey of ancient origins and profound spiritual connection. Pilgrims have the opportunity to immerse themselves in the rich traditions, history, and culture of Asturias and Galicia, connecting with local communities and fellow travelers from around the world. The Camino Primitivo also provides numerous opportunities for spiritual reflection and contemplation, with its stunning natural beauty and remote landscapes offering a serene backdrop for personal introspection and spiritual growth.

The Camino Inglés: A Tranquil Path of Maritime Beauty and Historical Significance

The Camino Inglés, or the English Way, is a lesser-known but historically significant pilgrimage route to Santiago de Compostela, starting from the port cities of Ferrol and A Coruña in northwestern Spain. This detailed exploration will uncover the highlights, challenges, and unique characteristics of the Camino Inglés, inviting pilgrims to embark on a journey of maritime beauty and cultural discovery.

Route Highlights

The Camino Inglés offers pilgrims a tranquil and scenic journey, with highlights including:

Ferrol: Pilgrims starting in Ferrol are greeted by the city's historic port, charming old town, and imposing San Felipe Castle, which offers panoramic views of the surrounding coastline.

A Coruña: Starting in A Coruña allows pilgrims to explore the city's picturesque waterfront, historic Roman lighthouse (Tower of Hercules), and vibrant cultural scene before setting out on their pilgrimage.

Coastal Scenery: Both routes of the Camino Inglés offer stunning views of the Galician coastline, with rugged cliffs, sandy beaches, and picturesque fishing villages dotting the landscape.

Pontedeume and Betanzos: These historic towns along the Camino Inglés are known for their medieval architecture, charming squares, and rich cultural heritage, providing pilgrims with a glimpse into Galicia's past.

Santiago de Compostela: The final destination of the Camino Inglés is the majestic Cathedral of Santiago de Compostela, where pilgrims gather to pay homage to Saint James and receive their compostela, or certificate of pilgrimage.

Challenges and Considerations

The Camino Inglés is relatively short compared to other routes, with the Ferrol route covering approximately 120 kilometers (75 miles) and the A Coruña route covering around 75 kilometers (47 miles). However, pilgrims should still be prepared for variable weather conditions, especially along the coastal sections where rain and wind can be common. Additionally, while the Camino Inglés is less crowded than other routes, pilgrims should still plan their journey carefully, ensuring they have adequate provisions and accommodations along the way.

Cultural and Historical Significance

The Camino Inglés holds historical significance as one of the traditional pilgrimage routes used by pilgrims from the British Isles and northern Europe to reach Santiago de Compostela. In the Middle Ages, pilgrims would travel by sea to the ports of Ferrol and A Coruña before embarking on the pilgrimage on foot. Today, the Camino Inglés continues to attract pilgrims seeking a more intimate and contemplative pilgrimage experience, with its maritime beauty and historical charm offering a unique perspective on the Camino de Santiago tradition.

The Via de la Plata: A Historic Journey Through Spain's Heartland

The Via de la Plata, also known as the Silver Way, is a historic pilgrimage route that spans the breadth of Spain, connecting the southern city of Seville to Santiago de Compostela in the north. This detailed exploration will uncover the highlights, challenges, and unique characteristics of the Via de la Plata, inviting pilgrims to embark on a journey of cultural richness and historical significance.

Route Highlights

The Via de la Plata offers pilgrims a diverse and captivating journey, with highlights including:

Seville: Pilgrims beginning their journey in Seville are captivated by the city's Moorish architecture, vibrant flamenco scene, and rich cultural heritage.

Mérida: This ancient Roman city is home to an impressive array of archaeological sites, including a well-preserved Roman theater, aqueduct, and bridge, providing pilgrims with a glimpse into Spain's rich history.

Cáceres: A UNESCO World Heritage site, Cáceres is renowned for its medieval old town, fortified walls, and historic architecture, offering pilgrims a step back in time to the Middle Ages.

Salamanca: Known for its prestigious university, stunning Plaza Mayor, and golden sandstone buildings, Salamanca is a highlight of the Via de la Plata, captivating pilgrims with its beauty and cultural significance.

Zamora: This historic city is home to a wealth of Romanesque architecture, including the stunning Zamora Cathedral, as well as a rich artistic heritage and vibrant cultural scene.

Santiago de Compostela: The final destination of the Via de la Plata is the majestic Cathedral of Santiago de Compostela, where pilgrims gather to pay homage to Saint James and receive their compostela, or certificate of pilgrimage.

Challenges and Considerations

The Via de la Plata is one of the longest and most challenging pilgrimage routes, covering approximately 1,000 kilometers (620 miles) from Seville to Santiago de Compostela. Pilgrims should be prepared for long distances, variable weather conditions, and rugged terrain, especially in the mountainous regions of northern Spain. Additionally, the infrastructure along the Via de la Plata is less developed compared to other routes, with fewer pilgrim accommodations and services along the way. Pilgrims should plan their journey carefully, ensuring they have adequate provisions and accommodations to meet their needs.

Cultural and Historical Significance

The Via de la Plata holds deep cultural and historical significance, following an ancient Roman road that was once used for trade and communication across the Iberian Peninsula. Along the route, pilgrims encounter a rich tapestry of history, culture, and architecture, from Roman ruins and medieval towns to Renaissance palaces and Baroque churches. The Via de la Plata also offers pilgrims the opportunity to connect with local communities, experience regional cuisine and traditions, and immerse themselves in the diverse cultures of Spain's heartland.

Camino Finisterre and Muxía: The Journey to the End of the Earth

The Camino Finisterre and Muxía, also known as the Camino de Fisterra, is an extension of the traditional Camino de Santiago pilgrimage route that takes pilgrims to the rugged coastline of Galicia, Spain, to the westernmost point of continental Europe. This detailed exploration will uncover the highlights, challenges, and unique characteristics of the Camino Finisterre and Muxía, inviting pilgrims to embark on a journey of spiritual reflection and awe-inspiring natural beauty.

Route Highlights

The Camino Finisterre and Muxía offers pilgrims a unique and awe-inspiring journey, with highlights including:

Santiago de Compostela: Pilgrims typically start their journey in Santiago de Compostela, where they visit the majestic Cathedral of Santiago and receive their compostela, or certificate of pilgrimage, before setting out on the extension to Finisterre and Muxía.

Finisterre: Known as the "end of the earth," Finisterre is the westernmost point of continental Europe and holds deep significance for pilgrims as a place of spiritual reflection and renewal. Pilgrims can visit the iconic Fisterra Lighthouse, explore the rugged coastline, and witness breathtaking sunsets over the Atlantic Ocean.

Muxía: Just a short distance from Finisterre lies the coastal town of Muxía, known for its stunning beaches, dramatic cliffs, and the legendary Sanctuary of the Virgin of the Boat. Pilgrims can visit the sanctuary, which is built on the site where the Virgin Mary is said to have appeared to the apostle Saint James, and take in the awe-inspiring views of the rugged coastline.

Challenges and Considerations
While the Camino Finisterre and Muxía is relatively short compared to other pilgrimage routes, covering approximately 90 kilometers (56 miles) from Santiago de Compostela to Finisterre and Muxía, it still presents its own set of challenges and considerations for pilgrims. The terrain can be rugged and hilly, with steep ascents and descents, especially along the coastal sections. Additionally, pilgrims should be prepared for variable weather conditions, especially along the exposed coastline, where wind and rain can be common. Pilgrims should plan their journey carefully, ensuring they have adequate provisions and accommodations along the way.

Cultural and Spiritual Significance
The Camino Finisterre and Muxía holds deep cultural and spiritual significance for pilgrims, offering a journey of introspection, reflection, and renewal. Finisterre, in particular, has been a sacred site for millennia, long before the arrival of Christianity, and continues to draw pilgrims seeking a deeper connection to the natural world and the divine. Muxía, with its

legendary sanctuary and stunning coastal landscapes, provides pilgrims with a sense of awe and wonder, inviting them to contemplate the mysteries of faith and the beauty of creation.

Comparing Routes: Difficulty, Scenery, and Highlights

The Camino de Santiago pilgrimage network offers a variety of routes, each with its own unique characteristics, challenges, and highlights. In this detailed exploration, we will compare several popular Camino routes based on difficulty, scenery, and highlights, providing pilgrims with valuable insights to help them choose the route that best suits their preferences and abilities.

Camino Francés

Difficulty: The Camino Francés covers approximately 780 kilometers (485 miles) from St. Jean Pied de Port in France to Santiago de Compostela in Spain. While the terrain is mostly manageable, there are some challenging sections, such as the ascent to O Cebreiro and the descent into Molinaseca. Pilgrims should be prepared for long distances between accommodations, especially in rural areas, and should consider training for endurance and strength to handle the daily walking distances.

Scenery: The Camino Francés offers diverse landscapes, from the lush green hills of the Pyrenees to the expansive plains of Castilla y León and the misty forests of Galicia. Pilgrims will pass through charming villages, medieval towns, and vineyard-covered hills, with highlights including the rolling landscapes of La Rioja, the historic city of Burgos with its

Gothic cathedral, and the picturesque village of Rabanal del Camino.

Highlights: Key highlights along the Camino Francés include the medieval city of Pamplona, famous for its running of the bulls during the San Fermín festival; the Gothic splendor of León's cathedral; the majestic Cruz de Ferro, a towering iron cross atop a hillside; and the iconic Cathedral of Santiago de Compostela, where pilgrims gather to pay homage to Saint James.

Camino Portugués

Difficulty: The Camino Portugués covers approximately 240 kilometers (150 miles) from Porto or Lisbon to Santiago de Compostela. The terrain is mostly flat, with some gradual climbs and descents along the way. While the route is generally less challenging than others, pilgrims should still be prepared for long days of walking and should consider training for endurance and stamina.

Scenery: The Camino Portugués offers diverse landscapes, from the historic cities of Porto and Coimbra to the lush green countryside of northern Portugal and Galicia. Pilgrims will pass through charming villages, vineyard-covered hillsides, and scenic coastal landscapes, with highlights including the picturesque town of Ponte de Lima, the historic city of Tui with its medieval cathedral, and the stunning coastline of Galicia.

Highlights: Key highlights along the Camino Portugués include the UNESCO-listed city of Porto, famous for its historic center and port wine production; the medieval town of Pontevedra with its stone streets and Gothic churches; the charming fishing village of Redondela; and the majestic Cathedral of Santiago de Compostela.

Camino del Norte

Difficulty: The Camino del Norte covers approximately 825 kilometers (513 miles) along the northern coast of Spain, from Irún to Santiago de Compostela. The terrain is rugged and challenging, with steep climbs, rocky paths, and variable weather conditions, especially along the coastal sections. Pilgrims should be prepared for long distances between accommodations and should consider training for strength and endurance.

Scenery: The Camino del Norte offers stunning coastal scenery, with panoramic views of the Bay of Biscay, rugged cliffs, and sandy beaches. Pilgrims will pass through charming fishing villages, lush green valleys, and dense forests, with highlights including the Basque Country's vibrant city of San Sebastián, the picturesque town of Llanes with its medieval architecture, and the rugged coastline of Asturias.

Highlights: Key highlights along the Camino del Norte include the Gothic splendor of Bilbao's Guggenheim Museum, the historic town of Gijón with its Roman ruins and sandy beaches, the charming fishing village of Luarca, and the majestic Cathedral of Santiago de Compostela.

Camino Primitivo

Difficulty: The Camino Primitivo covers approximately 320 kilometers (200 miles) from Oviedo to Santiago de Compostela. The terrain is rugged and challenging, with steep climbs, rocky paths, and remote stretches. Pilgrims should be prepared for long distances between accommodations and should consider training for endurance and stamina.

Scenery: The Camino Primitivo offers stunning mountain scenery, with panoramic views of the Asturian Mountains, lush green valleys, and remote villages. Pilgrims will pass through dense forests, picturesque meadows, and ancient oak groves, with highlights including the medieval city of Lugo with its well-preserved Roman walls, the picturesque village of Melide known for its pulpo a la gallega (Galician octopus), and the tranquil countryside of Galicia.

Highlights: Key highlights along the Camino Primitivo include the historic city of Oviedo with its pre-Romanesque churches, the charming town of Tineo with its medieval architecture, the stunning landscapes of Galicia's lush green valleys, and the majestic Cathedral of Santiago de Compostela.

Camino Inglés

Difficulty: The Camino Inglés covers approximately 120 kilometers (75 miles) from Ferrol or A Coruña to Santiago de Compostela. The terrain is relatively flat and well-marked, with shorter daily distances compared to other routes. While the Camino Inglés is generally considered easier in terms of terrain, pilgrims should still be prepared for long days of walking and should consider training for endurance and stamina.

Scenery: The Camino Inglés offers scenic countryside, charming villages, and historic cities. Pilgrims will pass through lush green landscapes, picturesque farmland, and tranquil forests, with highlights including the historic city of Ferrol with its naval heritage, the charming fishing village of Pontedeume, and the stunning coastal vistas of Finisterre and Muxía.

Highlights: Key highlights along the Camino Inglés include the historic city of A Coruña with its Roman lighthouse (Tower of Hercules), the medieval town of Betanzos with its well-preserved historic center, the picturesque countryside of Galicia, and the stunning coastal landscapes of Finisterre and Muxía.

Chapter 3: Accommodation and Services

Accommodation and services along the Camino de Santiago vary widely, offering pilgrims a range of options to suit their preferences and budget. Pilgrims can choose from a variety of accommodations, including albergues (hostels), guesthouses, hotels, and even camping sites along certain routes. Albergues are often the most affordable option, providing dormitory-style accommodation with shared facilities, while guesthouses and hotels offer more privacy and comfort at a higher cost. Along the Camino, pilgrims will also find a variety of services to support their journey, including restaurants, cafes, grocery stores, pharmacies, and medical facilities in larger towns and villages. Additionally, many albergues and pilgrim hostels offer communal kitchens, laundry facilities, and communal areas where pilgrims can rest, socialize, and share their experiences with fellow travelers, fostering a sense of camaraderie and community along the pilgrimage route.

Types of Accommodation on the Camino de Santiago

Accommodation options along the Camino de Santiago cater to the diverse needs and preferences of pilgrims, offering a range of choices to suit varying budgets, comfort levels, and travel styles. Here are the main types of accommodation available:

Albergues (Hostels)

Albergues are the most traditional and budget-friendly accommodation option along the Camino. These pilgrim hostels offer dormitory-style rooms with bunk beds, shared bathrooms, and communal facilities such as kitchens, dining areas, and laundry facilities. Albergues are typically run by municipalities, religious organizations, or private individuals, and provide pilgrims with a simple yet comfortable place to rest and socialize with fellow travelers. Some albergues operate on a donation basis, while others charge a nominal fee for overnight stays.

Guesthouses and Pensiones

For pilgrims seeking more privacy and comfort, guesthouses and pensiones offer private rooms with either shared or en-suite bathrooms. These accommodations range from simple family-run guesthouses to more upscale boutique hotels, providing pilgrims with a cozy and welcoming atmosphere. Guesthouses often include amenities such as complimentary breakfast, Wi-Fi, and personalized hospitality, making them a popular choice for pilgrims looking for a bit of luxury along the Camino.

Hotels and Paradores

Pilgrims with larger budgets or those seeking a higher level of comfort can opt to stay in hotels or paradores along the Camino. Hotels range from budget-friendly options to luxury establishments, offering amenities such as private rooms, en-suite bathrooms, room service, and on-site restaurants. Paradores are historic hotels often housed in renovated castles, monasteries, or palaces, providing pilgrims with a unique and memorable lodging experience. While hotels and paradores are typically more expensive than other accommodation options, they offer comfort, convenience, and exceptional service for pilgrims looking to indulge during their pilgrimage journey.

Camping

For pilgrims who prefer to sleep under the stars, camping is also an option along certain sections of the Camino. There are designated campgrounds and campsites located along the route, offering facilities such as tent pitches, bathrooms, showers, and cooking areas. Pilgrims should be prepared to carry their own camping gear, including tents, sleeping bags, and cooking equipment, as well as to adhere to Leave No Trace principles to minimize their environmental impact.

Alternative Accommodation

In addition to traditional lodging options, there are also alternative accommodation choices available to pilgrims along the Camino. These may include monasteries, convents, refugios (mountain huts), farm stays, and even private homes that open their doors to pilgrims. These unique accommodations provide pilgrims with a chance to experience the local culture, hospitality, and way of life along the Camino, adding an extra layer of authenticity and enrichment to their pilgrimage experience.

Albergues: Pilgrim Hostels, Hotels, Guesthouses, and Other Lodging Options

When embarking on the Camino de Santiago pilgrimage, choosing the right accommodation is crucial for a comfortable and enriching journey. From albergues (pilgrim hostels) to guesthouses and other lodging options, here's a detailed guide to help travelers navigate the diverse range of accommodations available along the pilgrimage route:

Albergues (Pilgrim Hostels)

Types: Albergues come in various forms, including municipal albergues, private albergues, and donativo (donation-based) albergues. Municipal albergues are often run by local authorities and offer basic facilities at a low cost. Private albergues, on the other hand, are operated by individuals, organizations, or religious institutions and may offer more amenities and services for a higher fee. Donativo albergues rely on pilgrims' contributions to sustain operations and foster a sense of community among travelers.

Amenities: Albergues typically provide dormitory-style accommodation with bunk beds or single beds, shared bathrooms, communal kitchens, and laundry facilities. Some may offer additional amenities such as Wi-Fi, communal areas for socializing, and pilgrim libraries.

Booking Tips: Municipal albergues usually operate on a first-come, first-served basis, while private albergues may accept reservations in advance. Donativo albergues may not accept reservations and rely on pilgrims' contributions upon arrival. Pilgrims should plan their daily stages accordingly and be prepared for different booking procedures depending on the type of albergue.

Guesthouses and Pensiones

Description: Guesthouses and pensiones offer private accommodation with varying levels of comfort and amenities. They are typically family-run establishments that provide a more personalized experience for pilgrims seeking privacy and comfort along the Camino.

Amenities: Guesthouses and pensiones may offer private or shared rooms with en-suite or shared bathrooms. They often include amenities such as breakfast, Wi-Fi, and personalized hospitality from the hosts. Some may also provide additional services such as laundry, luggage storage, and on-site dining options.

Booking Tips: Pilgrims can book guesthouses and pensiones in advance through their websites, by phone, or through online booking platforms. It's advisable to check availability and make reservations ahead of time, especially during peak pilgrimage seasons when accommodations may fill up quickly.

Hotels and Paradores

Description: Hotels and paradores provide upscale accommodation options for pilgrims seeking luxury and comfort during their journey. Hotels range from budget-friendly options to boutique establishments, while paradores are historic hotels often housed in renovated castles, monasteries, or palaces.

Amenities: Hotels offer private rooms with en-suite bathrooms, room service, on-site dining options, and additional amenities such as spa facilities, fitness centers, and swimming pools. Paradores provide a unique and memorable lodging experience with luxurious furnishings, gourmet cuisine, and exceptional service.

Booking Tips: Pilgrims can book hotels and paradores in advance through various booking channels, including online platforms, travel agencies, or directly through the hotel's website or reservation center. It's advisable to book early, especially for popular or high-demand locations along the Camino.

Alternative Accommodation Options

Description: In addition to traditional lodging options, pilgrims may also encounter alternative accommodation choices along the Camino, such as monasteries, convents, refugios (mountain huts), farm stays, and even private homes that open their doors to pilgrims.

Amenities: Alternative accommodations offer unique experiences and cultural immersion opportunities, with varying levels of comfort and amenities. Pilgrims may have the opportunity to stay in historic buildings, participate in communal meals or activities, and connect with local hosts and communities along the Camino.

Booking Tips: Alternative accommodations may have different booking procedures, ranging from reservations through official websites or booking platforms to contacting hosts directly by phone or email. Pilgrims should research and inquire about availability and booking requirements in advance, especially for more unconventional lodging options.

Comprehensive Guide to Culinary Experiences Along the Camino de Santiago

Embarking on the Camino de Santiago is not only a pilgrimage of the spirit but also a journey of culinary exploration through the diverse regions of Spain. Here's a detailed guide to where to eat along the Camino, including restaurants, cafes, and pilgrim menus, along with specific names and locations to help guide travelers on their journey:

Restaurants

Description: Restaurants along the Camino offer a plethora of culinary delights, ranging from cozy family-run taverns to upscale dining establishments. Each restaurant showcases the unique flavors and specialties of the region, providing pilgrims with an opportunity to indulge in authentic Spanish cuisine.

Names and Locations
Restaurante El Portalón - Burgos (Camino Francés)
Casa Marcelo - Santiago de Compostela (Camino Francés)
Restaurante A Taberna do Bispo - Porto (Camino Portugués)
Restaurante A Marola - Ribadeo (Camino del Norte)
Asador Etxebarri - Axpe (Camino del Norte)
Restaurante Casa Solla - Pontevedra (Camino Portugués)

Cafes and Bars

Description: Cafes and bars are abundant along the Camino, offering pilgrims a place to rest and refuel with refreshing beverages and light snacks. Whether seeking a morning coffee or an afternoon pick-me-up, pilgrims will find plenty of options to satisfy their cravings.

Names and Locations

Café Bar El Camino - Leon (Camino Francés)
Café Bar O Mesón - Sarria (Camino Francés)
Bar El Descanso - Vigo (Camino Portugués)
Café Bar As Mariñas - Cudillero (Camino del Norte)
Bar A Lareira - Betanzos (Camino Inglés)
Bar Igara - San Sebastián (Camino del Norte)

Pilgrim Menus (Menu del Peregrino)

Description: Pilgrim menus are a popular dining option for pilgrims along the Camino, offering a complete meal at an affordable price. These menus feature traditional Spanish dishes and provide pilgrims with a taste of the local cuisine.

Names and Locations

Bar Restaurante O Camiño - Portomarín (Camino Francés)
Mesón O Tapas - Lugo (Camino Primitivo)
Restaurante O Patio - Tui (Camino Portugués)
Bar El Peregrino - Ribadeo (Camino del Norte)
Restaurante O'Pote - Santiago de Compostela (Camino Francés)
Mesón do Pulpo - Melide (Camino Francés).

Navigating Groceries and Supplies Along the Camino de Santiago

As pilgrims embark on the Camino de Santiago, ensuring access to groceries and essential supplies is vital for a successful and comfortable journey. Here's a detailed guide to finding groceries and supplies along the way:

Supermarkets and Grocery Stores

Description: Supermarkets and grocery stores are scattered along the Camino route, particularly in larger towns and cities. These establishments offer a wide range of food items, beverages, snacks, and basic supplies for pilgrims to stock up on during their journey.

Locations: Pilgrims can find supermarkets and grocery stores in towns and villages along the Camino, often located near the main square or along the main thoroughfare. Larger cities along the route, such as Pamplona, Burgos, Leon, and Santiago de Compostela, boast multiple supermarkets and grocery chains for pilgrims to choose from.

Local Markets

Description: Local markets are a treasure trove of fresh produce, artisanal goods, and regional specialties, providing pilgrims with an authentic taste of the local cuisine and culture. These markets often feature vendors selling fruits, vegetables, cheeses, bread, pastries, cured meats, and other local delicacies.

Locations: Markets are typically held on specific days of the week in towns and villages along the Camino. Pilgrims can inquire about market days and locations at local tourist information centers or accommodations along the route. Popular markets include the Mercado de Abastos in Santiago de Compostela and the Mercado de la Boquería in Barcelona (on the Camino Catalán).

Convenience Stores and Mini-Markets

Description: Convenience stores and mini-markets are convenient stops for pilgrims to pick up quick snacks, beverages, and basic necessities along the Camino. These small establishments are often found in rural areas and provide essential items for pilgrims on the go.

Locations: Pilgrims can find convenience stores and mini-markets in almost every town and village along the Camino route, particularly in areas with limited access to larger supermarkets. These stores may be located near albergues, hostels, or along the main path of the Camino.

Pharmacies and Health Supply Stores

Description: Pharmacies and health supply stores offer essential medical supplies, toiletries, sunscreen, insect repellent, and over-the-counter medications for pilgrims in need of healthcare and personal care items along the Camino.

Locations: Pharmacies are prevalent in towns and cities along the Camino route, often recognizable by the iconic green cross sign. Pilgrims can also find health supply stores near hospitals, medical centers, or in commercial areas of larger towns.

Outdoor and Sporting Goods Stores

Description: Outdoor and sporting goods stores cater to the needs of pilgrims requiring hiking gear, footwear, backpacks, walking poles, and other outdoor equipment for their pilgrimage journey.

Locations: Outdoor stores are typically found in larger towns and cities along the Camino route, offering a variety of products and brands to suit pilgrims' preferences and budgets. Popular outdoor stores include Decathlon, Intersport, and specialized hiking shops.

Comprehensive Guide to Medical Services and Pharmacies Along the Camino de Santiago

Ensuring access to medical services and pharmacies is crucial for the health and well-being of pilgrims undertaking the Camino de Santiago pilgrimage. Here's a detailed guide to finding medical assistance and pharmacies along the way:

Medical Services

Description: Medical services along the Camino de Santiago encompass a range of healthcare facilities, including hospitals, clinics, emergency centers, and first aid stations. These facilities provide medical care and assistance to pilgrims in need of treatment for injuries, illnesses, or other health-related concerns.

Locations: Hospitals and larger medical centers are typically located in major towns and cities along the Camino route, offering comprehensive medical services and specialized care. Clinics and emergency centers may be found in smaller towns and villages, providing basic medical care and first aid to pilgrims. Additionally, some albergues and hostels may have staff trained in first aid or basic medical assistance.

Pharmacies

Description: Pharmacies along the Camino de Santiago provide essential medications, over-the-counter remedies, first aid supplies, toiletries, and personal care items for pilgrims in need of pharmaceutical assistance. Pharmacists offer professional advice and guidance on managing health conditions and treating minor ailments.

Locations: Pharmacies are prevalent in towns and cities along the Camino route, easily identifiable by the green cross sign displayed outside. They are typically located in commercial areas, near hospitals, medical centers, or along main thoroughfares. Additionally, some pharmacies may offer extended hours or after-hours emergency services for pilgrims in need of medication outside regular business hours.

Medical Assistance and Emergencies

Description: In the event of a medical emergency or serious injury along the Camino, pilgrims can seek immediate assistance by dialing the emergency services number (112) or contacting local authorities, albergue staff, or fellow pilgrims for help. Emergency medical services (EMS) provide rapid response and transportation to medical facilities for urgent care and treatment.

Precautions: Pilgrims are advised to carry a pilgrim credential (credencial del peregrino) with them at all times, as it contains important contact information for medical assistance and emergency services along the Camino route. It's also recommended to have travel insurance that covers medical expenses and emergency evacuation in case of unforeseen circumstances.

Health and Safety Tips

Preparation: Pilgrims should take precautions to maintain their health and well-being during the journey, including staying hydrated, wearing appropriate footwear and clothing, practicing sun safety, and taking breaks to rest and recuperate.

First Aid Kit: Pilgrims are encouraged to carry a basic first aid kit containing essentials such as adhesive bandages, antiseptic wipes, pain relievers, blister treatment, sunscreen, insect repellent, and any necessary prescription medications.

Medical Conditions: Pilgrims with pre-existing medical conditions should ensure they have an adequate supply of medications and consult with their healthcare provider before embarking on the Camino. It's also advisable to carry a medical alert card or bracelet indicating any allergies or medical conditions.

Chapter 4: Navigation and Waymarking

Navigation along the Camino de Santiago is facilitated by a network of well-marked trails and signage, known as "waymarking," which guide pilgrims along the pilgrimage route. These distinctive yellow arrows, scallop shells, and signs provide clear direction and reassurance to travelers, ensuring they stay on course and navigate the Camino with ease. Additionally, pilgrims can utilize guidebooks, maps, GPS devices, and smartphone apps to supplement waymarking and enhance their navigation experience, allowing them to navigate the diverse landscapes and terrain of the Camino with confidence and peace of mind.

Understanding the Camino's Waymarking System

The Camino de Santiago's waymarking system is a vital navigation tool that guides pilgrims along the pilgrimage routes, providing clear direction and reassurance throughout the journey. Here's a detailed overview of the Camino's waymarking system:

Yellow Arrows

Description: Yellow arrows are the most common and recognizable symbol used for waymarking along the Camino routes. These simple, painted arrows are typically found on walls, trees, poles, pavement, and other surfaces along the trail, guiding pilgrims in the right direction.

Purpose: Yellow arrows indicate the correct path to follow and reassure pilgrims that they are on the Camino route. They are strategically placed at intersections, crossroads, and key points along the way to ensure pilgrims stay on course and avoid getting lost.

Scallop Shells

Description: Scallop shells are another prominent symbol of the Camino de Santiago, representing the traditional emblem of pilgrims on the journey to Santiago de Compostela. These distinctive shells are often painted or engraved on signs, markers, and pavement along the Camino route.

Meaning: Scallop shells symbolize the pilgrimage experience and serve as a guide for pilgrims, leading them along the path to Santiago de Compostela. The direction of the scallop shell, whether pointing upward or downward, indicates the correct direction to follow along the trail.

Signage

Description: In addition to yellow arrows and scallop shells, signage along the Camino route provides further guidance and information for pilgrims. These signs may include directional signs indicating distances to towns and landmarks, trail markers with route names and symbols, and informational signs with historical or cultural information.

Types of Signs: Directional signs are typically found at intersections, forks in the road, and major landmarks, helping pilgrims navigate the route and make informed decisions about their journey. Trail markers with route symbols, such as the yellow arrow or scallop shell, confirm that pilgrims are on the right path and reassure them of their progress.

Additional Waymarking

Variations: While yellow arrows and scallop shells are the primary symbols used for waymarking along the Camino routes, pilgrims may encounter additional variations depending on the region and local customs. These may include other symbols, colors, or markers specific to certain trails or regions of the Camino.

Consistency: Despite variations, the waymarking system is designed to be consistent and easily recognizable, ensuring pilgrims can navigate the Camino routes with confidence and ease. Pilgrims are encouraged to familiarize themselves with the specific waymarking symbols and signs relevant to their chosen route before setting out on their journey.

Using Guidebooks, Maps, and GPS Devices

The Camino de Santiago, with its network of ancient pilgrimage routes, attracts thousands of pilgrims from around the world each year. While the journey is steeped in tradition and spirituality, modern technology has made navigation easier than ever before. In this guide, we'll explore the use of guidebooks, maps, and GPS services to help pilgrims navigate the Camino routes with confidence and ease.

Guidebooks

Overview: Guidebooks are invaluable resources for pilgrims embarking on the Camino de Santiago, offering detailed information on route options, accommodations, points of interest, historical and cultural sites, and practical tips for the journey.

Types of Guidebooks: There are numerous guidebooks available for the Camino, catering to different preferences and needs. Some focus on specific routes like the Camino Francés or the Camino del Norte, while others provide comprehensive coverage of multiple routes. Additionally, guidebooks may vary in format, including printed books, e-books, and online resources.

Contents: Guidebooks typically include route descriptions, maps, elevation profiles, accommodation listings, dining options, sightseeing recommendations, historical background, and practical advice on packing, budgeting, and transportation. They also provide insights into the pilgrimage experience and cultural significance of the Camino.

Recommendations: Pilgrims should choose guidebooks that align with their preferences, interests, and logistical needs. Popular guidebook series for the Camino include the Camino Guides by John Brierley, the Village to Village Guidebooks by Anna Dintaman and David Landis, and the Cicerone Guides.

Maps

Importance of Maps: Maps are essential tools for navigating the Camino de Santiago, providing visual representations of the routes, terrain, landmarks, and points of interest along the way. They help pilgrims plan their daily itinerary, track their progress, and make informed decisions about route options and detours.

Types of Maps: There are various types of maps available for the Camino, including printed maps, digital maps, online maps, and smartphone apps. Printed maps offer a tangible reference for offline navigation, while digital maps provide interactive features and real-time updates.

Features: Camino maps typically feature route markings, symbols, distances between towns, elevation profiles, accommodation symbols, dining options, and points of interest. Some maps also include information on water sources, rest areas, churches, and historical monuments.

Sources: Pilgrims can obtain maps from guidebooks, tourism offices, pilgrim associations, online retailers, and specialized map publishers. Many maps are available in multiple languages and formats to cater to international pilgrims.

GPS Services

Role of GPS Services: Global Positioning System (GPS) services play a crucial role in modern navigation along the Camino de Santiago, offering real-time location tracking, route guidance, and additional features to enhance the pilgrimage experience.

Types of GPS Services: There are several GPS services tailored specifically for the Camino, including dedicated GPS devices, smartphone apps, and online platforms. These services utilize GPS technology, satellite data, and mapping software to provide accurate positioning and navigation assistance.

Features: GPS services for the Camino offer a range of features, including route mapping, waypoint marking, offline navigation, distance tracking, elevation profiling, voice-guided directions, geolocation of amenities, and user-generated content such as reviews and tips.

Popular GPS Options: Some popular GPS options for the Camino include the Wikiloc app, the Maps.me app, the Buen Camino app, the Wise Pilgrim app, and dedicated GPS devices like the Garmin eTrex series or the Garmin GPSMAP series.

Using Guidebooks, Maps, and GPS Together

Integration: Pilgrims can maximize their navigation capabilities by using guidebooks, maps, and GPS services together in a complementary manner. Guidebooks provide detailed information and context, maps offer visual guidance and planning tools, and GPS services offer real-time positioning and navigation assistance.

Preparation: Before starting the Camino, pilgrims should familiarize themselves with their chosen guidebook, map, and GPS service, ensuring they understand the features, functionality, and coverage areas. It's also advisable to download offline maps and GPS data to ensure access in areas with limited connectivity.

On the Trail: While walking the Camino, pilgrims can refer to their guidebook for route descriptions, historical insights, and practical advice. Maps can be consulted for visual reference and planning, while GPS services can provide real-time location tracking and navigation assistance, especially at complex intersections or in unfamiliar terrain.

Flexibility: Pilgrims should maintain flexibility and use a combination of guidebooks, maps, and GPS services based on their preferences, needs, and circumstances. Some may prefer the convenience of digital navigation, while others may enjoy the tactile experience of using printed materials.

Tips for Staying on Track and Avoiding Common Pitfalls

Embarking on the Camino de Santiago is a transformative journey filled with adventure, camaraderie, and spiritual discovery. However, navigating the ancient pilgrimage routes can present challenges and pitfalls for pilgrims along the way. In this guide, we'll provide comprehensive tips for staying on track and avoiding common pitfalls, ensuring a safe, fulfilling, and enriching pilgrimage experience.

Plan Your Route

Research: Before setting out on the Camino, research and plan your route carefully. Consider factors such as distance, terrain, accommodations, and points of interest along the way. Choose a route that aligns with your fitness level, preferences, and time frame for the journey.

Consult Guidebooks and Maps: Utilize guidebooks, maps, and online resources to familiarize yourself with the route, including trail markings, landmarks, and potential challenges. Pay attention to elevation profiles, distances between towns, and services available along the route.

Consider Alternate Routes: Be prepared to adapt your route as needed based on weather conditions, trail closures, or personal circumstances. Familiarize yourself with alternate paths and transportation options in case of emergencies or unforeseen circumstances.

Stay Oriented with Waymarking

Understand Waymarking Symbols: Familiarize yourself with the common waymarking symbols used along the Camino, including yellow arrows, scallop shells, and trail markers. These symbols provide guidance and reassurance, indicating the correct path to follow.

Pay Attention to Signs: Stay vigilant and observant of waymarking signs and symbols along the trail. Look for markers at intersections, forks in the road, and key decision points to ensure you stay on course.

Trust Your Instincts: While waymarking provides valuable guidance, trust your instincts and common sense when navigating the Camino. If a trail seems unclear or unfamiliar, take a moment to reassess your surroundings and consult your map or GPS device for guidance.

Pace Yourself

Start Slowly: Pace yourself at the beginning of your journey to avoid burnout and injury. Take time to acclimate to the physical demands of walking long distances each day, gradually increasing your pace as your strength and stamina improve.

Listen to Your Body: Pay attention to your body's signals and listen to any signs of fatigue, discomfort, or pain. Take regular breaks to rest, stretch, hydrate, and refuel throughout the day to prevent overexertion and injury.

Set Realistic Goals: Establish realistic daily mileage goals based on your fitness level, terrain, and the overall duration of your journey. Be flexible and adjust your goals as needed to accommodate unforeseen challenges or changes in your circumstances.

Pack Wisely

Lighten Your Load: Pack light and only carry essential items to reduce the physical strain of walking long distances each day. Prioritize lightweight, multi-purpose gear and clothing that is durable, breathable, and suitable for varying weather conditions.

Essential Items: Pack essential items such as a sturdy backpack, comfortable hiking shoes, weather-appropriate clothing, a lightweight sleeping bag, toiletries, a first aid kit, sunscreen, a refillable water bottle, snacks, and a pilgrim credential.

Leave Non-Essentials Behind: Avoid overpacking by leaving unnecessary items at home or sending them ahead to your final destination. Consider sharing communal items such as toiletries and guidebooks with fellow pilgrims to lighten your load.

Embrace the Pilgrimage Experience

Stay Present: Embrace the journey and stay present in the moment, focusing on the sights, sounds, and sensations of the Camino. Take time to appreciate the natural beauty, cultural heritage, and spiritual significance of the places you encounter along the way.

Cultivate Resilience: Approach challenges and setbacks with resilience, patience, and a positive mindset. Use setbacks as opportunities for growth and learning, and draw upon the support of fellow pilgrims, local communities, and your own inner strength to overcome obstacles.

Celebrate Milestones: Celebrate milestones and achievements along the Camino, whether it's reaching a new town, conquering a difficult ascent, or experiencing a moment of personal reflection and insight. Cherish the memories and experiences that make the pilgrimage journey unique and meaningful to you.

Connect with Fellow Pilgrims

Build Community: Take advantage of the opportunity to connect with fellow pilgrims from around the world, sharing stories, experiences, and camaraderie along the way. Join pilgrim dinners, participate in communal activities, and engage in meaningful conversations to foster connections and friendships.

Offer and Receive Support: Be open to offering and receiving support from fellow pilgrims, whether it's lending a listening ear, sharing resources, or offering assistance in times of need. The Camino community is known for its spirit of generosity, compassion, and solidarity, and embracing this ethos can enrich your pilgrimage experience.

Respect Diversity: Embrace the diversity of the Camino community and respect the different backgrounds, beliefs, and experiences of your fellow pilgrims. Practice tolerance, empathy, and mutual respect, fostering an inclusive and welcoming environment for all who walk the Camino.

Chapter 5: Daily Life on the Camino

Daily life on the Camino de Santiago is a rich tapestry of experiences, rhythms, and interactions that blend the physical challenges of walking with moments of reflection, camaraderie, and cultural immersion. Each day begins with the sound of footsteps on the trail, as pilgrims set out before dawn to beat the heat and make progress towards their next destination. Along the way, pilgrims traverse diverse landscapes, from rolling hills and verdant valleys to bustling towns and tranquil villages, encountering ancient churches, medieval bridges, and picturesque countryside vistas. Breaks for rest and refreshment punctuate the journey, with pilgrims pausing at roadside cafes, rustic taverns, and shaded picnic spots to replenish their energy and share stories with fellow travelers. Evenings are spent in communal albergues, where pilgrims from around the world come together to prepare meals, tend to their weary feet, and swap tales of the day's adventures before drifting off to sleep, lulled by the collective rhythm of shared dreams and aspirations along the Camino.

A Typical Day as a Pilgrim on the Camino de Santiago

Every day as a pilgrim on the Camino de Santiago is a unique blend of physical exertion, cultural immersion, and spiritual contemplation. Here's a detailed breakdown of what a typical day might look like:

Early Morning

Wake-Up Call: Pilgrims rise before dawn, often to the sound of alarm clocks or the gentle rustling of fellow travelers preparing to depart. Some choose to start walking while it's still dark to avoid the heat of the day, while others prefer to wait until sunrise for better visibility.

Preparation: Pilgrims pack up their belongings, repack their backpacks, and gather any last-minute essentials for the day ahead. This might include filling water bottles, applying sunscreen, and grabbing a quick breakfast of fruit, nuts, or energy bars.

Morning Walk

Setting Out: As the sun begins to rise, pilgrims set out on the trail, their footsteps echoing on the quiet morning air. The path stretches out before them, winding through forests, fields, and quaint villages as they make their way towards their next destination.

Scenic Views: Along the way, pilgrims are treated to breathtaking views of the surrounding countryside, with the changing light casting a golden glow over the landscape. They pause to admire ancient churches, medieval bridges, and other historic landmarks, soaking in the rich cultural heritage of the Camino.

Midday Break

Rest and Refreshment: By mid-morning, pilgrims begin to feel the effects of the day's journey, and they take a break to rest and refuel. They stop at roadside cafes, village squares, or shaded rest areas to enjoy a leisurely snack or meal, savoring the local cuisine and camaraderie of fellow travelers.

Social Interaction: The midday break is also a time for social interaction, as pilgrims swap stories, share tips, and offer encouragement to one another. Language barriers fade away as friendships are forged over shared experiences and mutual support.

Afternoon Trek

Continued Journey: Energized by their break, pilgrims resume their journey along the Camino, pressing onward towards their final destination for the day. The afternoon trek is often the most challenging, with fatigue setting in and the sun beating down overhead.

Mindful Walking: Despite the physical demands, pilgrims approach the afternoon trek with mindfulness and determination, focusing on each step and embracing the rhythm of their breath. They draw strength from the collective energy of the Camino community and the sense of purpose that propels them forward.

Arrival at Destination

Arrival: As the afternoon wears on, pilgrims arrive at their chosen destination for the day, whether it's a bustling city, a quaint village, or a remote rural outpost. They feel a sense of accomplishment and relief as they remove their backpacks and pause to catch their breath.

Accommodation: Pilgrims check into their accommodations for the night, whether it's a pilgrim hostel (albergue), guesthouse, hotel, or private lodging. They may choose to rest and recuperate before exploring the local area or participating in communal activities organized by the albergue.

Evening Routine

Dinner and Reflection: As evening falls, pilgrims gather for dinner, either at their accommodations or at a nearby restaurant or communal dining hall. They share a hearty meal and lively conversation, reflecting on the day's highlights and challenges, and exchanging plans for the days ahead.

Rest and Rejuvenation: After dinner, pilgrims tend to their weary bodies, tending to blisters, stretching sore muscles, and taking hot showers to refresh themselves. They may spend time journaling, meditating, or simply relaxing before retiring to bed, lulled to sleep by the gentle rhythm of the Camino and the promise of new adventures awaiting them tomorrow.

Camino Etiquette and Traditions

Embarking on the Camino de Santiago is not just a physical journey; it's also an opportunity to immerse oneself in a rich tapestry of traditions and practices that have been passed down through generations of pilgrims. From respecting local customs to embracing the spirit of camaraderie, observing etiquette and traditions is an integral part of the pilgrimage experience. In this guide, we'll delve into the intricacies of Camino etiquette and traditions, offering insights and advice to help pilgrims navigate the cultural landscape of the Camino with grace and respect.

Respect for Local Customs and Culture

Cultural Sensitivity: Pilgrims should approach the Camino with an open mind and a willingness to embrace the customs and traditions of the regions they pass through. This includes respecting local customs, traditions, and cultural norms, such as greetings, gestures, and dress codes.

Language: While English is widely spoken along the Camino, pilgrims should make an effort to learn basic phrases in the local language (Spanish, Basque, Galician, etc.) as a sign of respect and cultural appreciation. Simple greetings, expressions of gratitude, and polite requests go a long way in fostering positive interactions with locals.

Pilgrim Credentials and Compostelas

Pilgrim Credentials: Pilgrims are encouraged to obtain a pilgrim credential (credencial del peregrino) before setting out on the Camino. This document serves as a passport for pilgrims, allowing them to collect stamps (sellos) at churches, albergues, and other designated locations along the route as proof of their journey.

Compostelas: Upon reaching Santiago de Compostela, pilgrims can present their completed pilgrim credentials at the Pilgrim's Office to receive a Compostela, a certificate of completion of the pilgrimage. To qualify for a Compostela, pilgrims must have walked at least the last 100 kilometers on foot or cycled the last 200 kilometers to Santiago.

Albergue Etiquette

Respect Quiet Hours: Albergues (pilgrim hostels) typically have designated quiet hours, usually from 10 pm to 6 am, to ensure that pilgrims can rest and recuperate without disturbance. Pilgrims should respect these quiet hours by refraining from loud conversations, using electronic devices, or engaging in disruptive behavior during this time.

Cleanliness and Consideration: Pilgrims should strive to maintain cleanliness and tidiness in shared spaces, including dormitories, bathrooms, and communal areas. This includes keeping personal belongings organized, disposing of trash properly, and leaving common areas as they found them for the next pilgrims.

Pilgrim's Meal (Menu del Peregrino)

Community Dining: Many albergues and restaurants along the Camino offer a special pilgrim's meal (Menu del Peregrino) for pilgrims to enjoy together in a communal setting. This simple and affordable meal typically includes a starter, main course, dessert, bread, and a beverage, allowing pilgrims to refuel and connect with fellow travelers.

Participation: Pilgrims are encouraged to participate in pilgrim meals as a way to foster camaraderie and camaraderie with fellow travelers. Sharing a meal with other pilgrims provides an opportunity to exchange stories, share tips, and forge friendships that can last a lifetime.

Buen Camino

Meaning: "Buen Camino" is a common greeting among pilgrims on the Camino de Santiago, meaning "Good Journey" or "Have a Good Camino." It is used as a greeting, farewell, or expression of encouragement and support, conveying well-wishes for a safe and fulfilling pilgrimage experience.

Usage: Pilgrims exchange "Buen Camino" with one another as they pass on the trail, offering a sense of connection and solidarity with fellow travelers. The phrase serves as a reminder of the shared purpose and collective spirit that unites pilgrims on their journey to Santiago.

Pilgrim's Blessing

Receiving Blessings: Along the Camino, pilgrims may have the opportunity to receive blessings from clergy, monks, or local residents at churches, chapels, or pilgrimage sites along the route. These blessings are often offered as a gesture of goodwill and spiritual support for pilgrims on their journey.

Appreciation: Pilgrims are encouraged to receive blessings with gratitude and reverence, regardless of their religious beliefs or affiliations. Accepting blessings with an open heart and a spirit of humility can deepen the spiritual significance of the pilgrimage experience and foster a sense of connection to the sacred traditions of the Camino.

Leaving No Trace

Environmental Responsibility: Pilgrims should adhere to the principles of Leave No Trace to minimize their impact on the natural environment and preserve the beauty of the Camino for future generations. This includes packing out trash, avoiding littering, staying on designated trails, and respecting wildlife and natural habitats.

Cultural Heritage: In addition to environmental conservation, pilgrims should also respect and protect the cultural heritage of the Camino, including historic landmarks, archaeological sites, and sacred monuments. Pilgrims should refrain from defacing or removing artifacts and refrain from engaging in activities that may damage or disrupt these cultural treasures.

Making Connections: Camino Companions and Community

The Camino de Santiago is not just a pilgrimage; it's a journey of connection – with oneself, with fellow pilgrims, and with the world around us. Along the ancient trails of the Camino, pilgrims have the opportunity to forge deep and meaningful connections with a diverse community of travelers from around the globe. From chance encounters on the trail to shared meals in albergues, these connections enrich the pilgrimage experience and remind us of the power of human connection in our shared quest for meaning and purpose. In this guide, we'll explore the art of making connections on the Camino, from forming bonds with fellow pilgrims to embracing the spirit of community along the way.

Embracing Camino Companionship

Chance Encounters: One of the most magical aspects of the Camino is the serendipitous nature of meeting fellow pilgrims along the way. Whether walking alone or in a group, pilgrims have the opportunity to connect with others from diverse backgrounds, cultures, and walks of life.

Shared Experiences: As pilgrims walk side by side on the trail, they share in the physical challenges, emotional highs, and spiritual insights of the journey. These shared experiences create a bond that transcends language barriers and cultural differences, fostering a sense of camaraderie and solidarity among pilgrims.

Engaging in Meaningful Conversations

Openness and Vulnerability: The Camino provides a safe and supportive space for pilgrims to engage in deep and meaningful conversations about life, faith, and personal growth. Pilgrims often find themselves opening up to strangers in ways they never imagined, sharing their hopes, fears, and dreams with newfound friends.

Active Listening: Listening is a crucial skill on the Camino, as pilgrims learn to listen not only with their ears but also with their hearts. By actively listening to the stories and experiences of fellow pilgrims, we can gain valuable insights into our own journey and cultivate empathy and understanding for others.

Sharing Meals and Stories

Pilgrim's Meals: One of the highlights of the Camino experience is sharing meals with fellow pilgrims in communal dining halls or albergues. These pilgrim meals, known as "Menu del Peregrino," provide an opportunity for pilgrims to come together as a community, break bread, and share stories from the road.

Cultural Exchange: Pilgrim meals are not just about nourishing the body; they're also about nourishing the soul. As pilgrims share food, laughter, and conversation, they also share their cultural heritage, traditions, and values, creating a rich tapestry of diversity and unity.

Offering and Receiving Support

Acts of Kindness: The Camino is a place where simple acts of kindness can have a profound impact on our journey. Whether it's offering a helping hand to a fellow pilgrim in need, sharing resources, or offering words of encouragement, small gestures of kindness can create ripple effects of positivity along the trail.

Mutual Support: Pilgrims often form bonds of friendship and mutual support as they navigate the challenges of the Camino together. Whether it's walking together for a stretch of the trail, lending a listening ear, or offering practical assistance, pilgrims have each other's backs every step of the way. Respecting Boundaries and Differences:

Individual Journeys: While the Camino is a communal experience, it's also a deeply personal journey for each pilgrim. It's important to respect the boundaries and differences of fellow travelers, recognizing that everyone is on their own unique path with their own reasons for walking.

Cultural Sensitivity: Pilgrims should be mindful of cultural differences and sensitivities when interacting with others on the Camino. This includes respecting personal space, avoiding intrusive questions, and refraining from making assumptions about others based on their background or beliefs.

Cultivating Gratitude and Appreciation

Gratitude Practices: Cultivating gratitude is an essential practice on the Camino, as pilgrims learn to appreciate the small joys and blessings of each day. Whether it's a breathtaking sunrise, a kind word from a stranger, or a warm meal at the end of a long day, there is always something to be thankful for on the Camino.

Appreciation for Community: By embracing the spirit of community on the Camino, pilgrims come to appreciate the interconnectedness of all beings and the power of human connection to uplift and inspire. Each encounter, whether fleeting or lasting, leaves an indelible mark on our hearts and reminds us of the beauty and richness of the human experience.

Leaving a Positive Legacy

Paying It Forward: As pilgrims complete their journey and return home, they carry with them the memories, lessons, and connections forged on the Camino. By embodyingthe values of kindness, compassion, and community in their everyday lives, pilgrims can leave a positive legacy that extends far beyond the boundaries of the trail.

Spreading Light: Just as a single candle can illuminate the darkness, so too can the light of our actions and intentions shine brightly in the world. By spreading kindness, love, and goodwill wherever we go, we cancreate a ripple effect of positivity that touches the lives of others and illuminates the path ahead. Whether it's offering a helping hand to someone in need, sharing a smile with a stranger, or speaking words of encouragement and support, each act of kindness has the power to brighten someone's day and uplift their spirits. In a world often filled with challenges and uncertainties, the simple yet profound act of spreading light reminds us of the inherent goodness within each of us and the transformative impact we can have on the world around us. As we journey through life, let us be beacons of light, radiating warmth, compassion, and hope to all we encounter, and inspiring others to do the same. Together, we can create a brighter, more beautiful world for ourselves and future generations to come.

Dealing with Challenges and Overcoming Obstacles on the Camino

Embarking on the Camino de Santiago is a transformative journey filled with moments of joy, discovery, and personal growth. However, like any pilgrimage, the Camino also presents its share of challenges and obstacles along the way. From physical exhaustion to emotional upheaval, pilgrims may encounter various difficulties that test their resilience and determination. In this detailed guide, we explore common challenges faced by pilgrims on the Camino and offer strategies for overcoming them with grace and perseverance.

Physical Challenges

Fatigue and Exhaustion: Walking long distances day after day can take a toll on the body, leading to fatigue and exhaustion. To overcome physical fatigue, it's essential to listen to your body, take regular breaks, and pace yourself accordingly. Proper rest, hydration, and nutrition are also vital for maintaining energy levels and preventing burnout.

Blisters and Foot Pain: Blisters and foot pain are common ailments experienced by pilgrims due to repetitive motion and friction from walking. To prevent blisters, wear well-fitting, moisture-wicking socks and shoes, and use blister prevention techniques such as applying moleskin or using lubricants like Vaseline on hot spots. Carry a first aid kit with blister treatment supplies and address any foot discomfort promptly to avoid worsening injuries.

Emotional Challenges

Loneliness and Isolation: The Camino can be a solitary journey, especially for solo travelers or those walking during quieter seasons. Feelings of loneliness and isolation may arise, particularly when facing long stretches of solitude on the trail. To combat loneliness, reach out to fellow pilgrims, participate in communal activities such as pilgrim dinners or group gatherings, and stay connected with loved ones through phone calls or messages.

Homesickness and Emotional Turmoil: Being away from familiar surroundings and support systems can trigger feelings of homesickness and emotional turmoil. Allow yourself to experience and acknowledge these emotions without judgment, and seek solace in the beauty of nature, the kindness of fellow pilgrims, and the spiritual connection of the Camino. Journaling, meditation, and seeking support from fellow pilgrims or hospitaleros can also help process and navigate challenging emotions.

Navigation and Wayfinding Challenges

Getting Lost: Navigation can be challenging, especially in rural areas with limited signage or when relying on maps or guidebooks. To avoid getting lost, familiarize yourself with route markers and trail signs, carry a detailed map or GPS device, and consult guidebooks or fellow pilgrims for directions when needed. Trust your instincts and don't hesitate to ask for help from locals or other pilgrims if you're unsure of the way.

Language Barriers: Language barriers may pose challenges, particularly for pilgrims who are not fluent in Spanish or other local languages. Learning basic phrases and greetings in the local language can facilitate communication and foster connections with locals and fellow pilgrims. Carry a phrasebook or language translation app for assistance, and don't be afraid to use gestures or nonverbal communication to convey your needs.

Spiritual and Existential Challenges

Doubt and Questioning: The Camino often prompts deep introspection and soul-searching, leading pilgrims to confront doubts, fears, and existential questions about life's purpose and meaning. Embrace these moments of introspection as opportunities for growth and self-discovery, and trust in the transformative power of the Camino journey to provide clarity and insight.

Spiritual Crisis: Pilgrims may experience spiritual crises or existential angst as they grapple with their beliefs, values, and sense of identity. Seek solace in the spiritual and sacred sites along the Camino, such as cathedrals, churches, and ancient monuments, and engage in contemplative practices such as prayer, meditation, or quiet reflection to nourish your soul and find inner peace.

Practical Challenges

Accommodation and Logistics: Securing accommodation, especially during peak seasons, can be challenging, requiring careful planning and flexibility. Book accommodations in advance whenever possible, but be prepared to adapt your plans based on availability and circumstances. Carry a lightweight sleeping bag and consider alternative lodging options such as albergues, hostels, or pilgrim refuges if needed.

Budgeting and Finances: Managing finances on the Camino requires careful budgeting and resourcefulness. Keep track of expenses, prioritize essential purchases, and take advantage of cost-saving measures such as cooking meals at albergue kitchens or sharing expenses with fellow pilgrims. Be prepared for unexpected costs or emergencies by carrying a contingency fund and having access to backup resources if needed.

Strategies for Overcoming Challenges

Stay Flexible and Adapt: Embrace the unpredictable nature of the Camino and be prepared to adapt your plans and expectations as needed. Flexibility is key to navigating challenges and seizing opportunities for growth and exploration along the way.

Draw Strength from the Camino Community: Lean on the support and camaraderie of fellow pilgrims, who share a common bond and understanding of the pilgrimage experience. Seek guidance, encouragement, and companionship from the Camino community, and offer support to others in return.

Practice Self-Compassion: Be gentle with yourself and practice self-compassion during moments of struggle or setback. Acknowledge your efforts and accomplishments, celebrate small victories, and cultivate resilience by treating yourself with kindness and understanding.

Focus on the Present Moment: Stay grounded in the present moment and focus on the here and now, rather than dwelling on past regrets or worrying about future uncertainties. Mindfulness practices such as deep breathing, body scanning, or walking meditation can help center your mind and body, fostering a sense of calm and clarity amidst challenges.

Chapter 6: Camino Culture and History

Camino Culture and History are intricately woven into the fabric of the pilgrimage experience, enriching the journey with centuries of tradition, spirituality, and heritage. Dating back to the Middle Ages, the Camino de Santiago has been a sacred pilgrimage route for countless travelers seeking spiritual enlightenment, redemption, and adventure. Along the Camino, pilgrims encounter a rich tapestry of cultural landmarks, including medieval cathedrals, historic monasteries, and ancient pilgrimage sites, each steeped in centuries of lore and legend. From the iconic scallop shell symbol to the traditional rituals of the Camino, such as receiving a pilgrim's blessing or attending a pilgrim's mass, every step along the trail is infused with the echoes of pilgrims past and the timeless rhythms of pilgrimage tradition. As pilgrims walk in the footsteps of those who have gone before, they become part of a living legacy that transcends time and connects them to a vibrant community of pilgrims spanning centuries and continents, united by a shared reverence for the sacred journey of the Camino de Santiago.

The Historical Significance of the Camino de Santiago

The historical significance of the Camino de Santiago is profound, spanning over a millennium of cultural, religious, and social evolution. Originating in the early Middle Ages, the Camino de Santiago emerged as one of the most important Christian pilgrimage routes, drawing believers from across Europe to the tomb of the apostle St. James in Santiago de Compostela, Spain. The discovery of the apostle's remains in the 9th century transformed Santiago de Compostela into a major pilgrimage destination, rivaling Jerusalem and Rome in its religious significance. The Camino served as a catalyst for cultural exchange, fostering the spread of ideas, art, and architecture across Europe, and played a pivotal role in the development of medieval European society. Along the route, pilgrims encountered a network of monasteries, hospitals, and churches, established to provide spiritual guidance, hospitality, and care for weary travelers. The Camino also served as a symbol of unity and identity for the diverse communities that flourished along its path, transcending linguistic, cultural, and political boundaries to create a shared sense of purpose and belonging among pilgrims. Despite fluctuations in popularity over the centuries, the Camino de Santiago has endured as a testament to the enduring power of faith, pilgrimage, and human connection, continuing to inspire millions of pilgrims from around the world to embark on their own journey of self-discovery and spiritual renewal along its ancient trails.

The Religious Aspects of the Camino de Santiago: A Spiritual Journey of Faith and Reflection

The Camino de Santiago, often referred to as the Way of St. James, is deeply rooted in religious tradition and spirituality, drawing pilgrims from diverse faith backgrounds to embark on a journey of faith, self-discovery, and spiritual renewal. From its origins as a Christian pilgrimage route to its modern-day significance as a symbol of interfaith dialogue and spiritual exploration, the Camino is imbued with layers of religious significance that resonate with pilgrims of all beliefs. In this comprehensive guide, we'll delve into the religious aspects of the Camino de Santiago, exploring its historical context, sacred sites, spiritual practices, and the profound impact it has on pilgrims' faith journeys.

Historical Context

Early Christian Tradition: The Camino de Santiago traces its origins back to the early Middle Ages when the tomb of the apostle St. James the Greater was discovered in Santiago de Compostela, Spain. Pilgrims began flocking to the site to pay homage to St. James and seek spiritual blessings, sparking the development of pilgrimage routes across Europe and the establishment of pilgrimage infrastructure along the Camino.

Medieval Pilgrimage Boom: During the medieval period, the Camino de Santiago experienced a surge in popularity, attracting pilgrims from all walks of life, including kings, knights, clergy, and commoners. The journey to Santiago became a form of penance, pilgrimage, and spiritual quest, offering believers the opportunity to atone for sins, seek healing, and deepen their relationship with God.

Sacred Sites Along the Camino

Cathedral of Santiago de Compostela: The culmination of the Camino journey is the majestic Cathedral of Santiago de Compostela, which houses the shrine of St. James the Greater. Pilgrims gather in the cathedral's grand nave to pay homage to the apostle, attend pilgrim masses, and receive the traditional pilgrim's blessing known as the "Botafumeiro."

Sanctuaries and Chapels: Along the Camino, pilgrims encounter a multitude of sanctuaries, chapels, and shrines dedicated to various saints and religious figures. These sacred sites serve as places of prayer, reflection, and spiritual contemplation, offering pilgrims opportunities for quiet introspection and communion with the divine.

Crosses and Waymarkers: Throughout the Camino, pilgrims encounter crosses, waymarkers, and other religious symbols that guide their journey and mark significant milestones along the route. These symbols serve as reminders of the spiritual significance of the pilgrimage and inspire pilgrims to persevere through challenges and obstacles.

Spiritual Practices and Rituals

Prayer and Meditation: Prayer and meditation are central to the spiritual experience of the Camino, providing pilgrims with opportunities for communion with the divine and inner reflection. Whether reciting traditional prayers, practicing mindfulness meditation, or engaging in silent contemplation, pilgrims use prayer as a means of seeking guidance, solace, and spiritual renewal.

Participation in Pilgrim Masses: Pilgrim masses are an integral part of the Camino experience, offering pilgrims the opportunity to come together in worship and celebration. Pilgrim masses are held daily along the Camino, often in historic churches and cathedrals, and feature special blessings for pilgrims, including the "Pilgrim's Prayer" and the "Pilgrim's Blessing."

Themes of Redemption and Renewal

Penance and Forgiveness: For many pilgrims, the Camino de Santiago is a journey of penance and reconciliation, offering them the opportunity to seek forgiveness for past wrongs and make amends for their sins. Through acts of contrition, confession, and acts of service, pilgrims embark on a path of spiritual renewal and redemption, seeking to heal the wounds of the past and embrace a future of grace and mercy.

Transformation and Renewal: The Camino is also a journey of transformation and renewal, inviting pilgrims to embark on a path of self-discovery and personal growth. Through the challenges and trials of the pilgrimage journey, pilgrims confront their limitations, overcome their fears, and emerge renewed and empowered to live lives of purpose, meaning, and service.

Interfaith Dialogue and Inclusivity

Beyond Christianity: While the Camino de Santiago has its roots in Christian tradition, it has evolved into a pilgrimage route that welcomes people of all faiths and spiritual beliefs. Pilgrims from diverse religious backgrounds, including Judaism, Islam, Buddhism, and Hinduism, walk the Camino, each seeking their own spiritual truths and insights.

Universal Themes: Despite their differences, pilgrims on the Camino share a common humanity and a shared quest for meaning, purpose, and connection. Through the shared experience of pilgrimage, pilgrims transcend religious boundaries and engage in dialogue, mutual respect, and understanding, fostering a spirit of interfaith harmony and cooperation.

Impact on Pilgrims' Faith Journeys

Deepening of Faith: For many pilgrims, the Camino de Santiago is a transformative spiritual experience that deepens their faith and strengthens their relationship with God. Through prayer, reflection, and encounters with sacred sites and symbols, pilgrims experience moments of divine grace and revelation that inspire them to live lives of greater faithfulness, compassion, and devotion.

Integration of Faith and Life: The lessons learned and insights gained on the Camino often have a lasting impact on pilgrims' lives long after they return home. Pilgrims are challenged to integrate their faith experiences into their daily lives, living out the values of the Camino – humility, kindness, and solidarity in their relationships, work, and communities.

Cultural Highlights Along the Way: Enhancing the Pilgrim Experience on the Camino de Santiago

The Camino de Santiago is not just a physical journey; it is a cultural odyssey that takes pilgrims through centuries of history, tradition, and heritage. As pilgrims traverse the ancient trails of the Camino, they encounter a myriad of cultural highlights, including historic towns, UNESCO World Heritage sites, and architectural marvels that offer insights into the rich tapestry of the regions through which they pass. In this comprehensive guide, we will explore the significance of cultural highlights along the Camino and how they enrich the pilgrimage experience for pilgrims from around the world.

Historical Towns and Cities

Leon: The historic city of Leon, with its magnificent Gothic cathedral and charming old town, is a highlight along the Camino Francés. Pilgrims can explore the city's rich history and cultural heritage, visiting landmarks such as the Casa Botines, designed by renowned architect Antoni Gaudí, and the San Isidoro Basilica, home to the Royal Pantheon.

Burgos: Another cultural gem along the Camino Francés is the city of Burgos, known for its stunning cathedral, a UNESCO World Heritage site, and its medieval architecture. Pilgrims can wander through the city's cobblestone streets, marvel at the majestic Arco de Santa María, and visit the historic Monastery of Las Huelgas.

UNESCO World Heritage Sites

Santiago de Compostela: The culmination of the Camino journey, Santiago de Compostela, is a UNESCO World Heritage site renowned for its stunning cathedral, historic old town, and vibrant cultural scene. Pilgrims can attend the pilgrim's mass at the cathedral, visit the tomb of St. James, and explore the city's museums, galleries, and traditional markets.

Basilica of San Isidoro, Leon: The Basilica of San Isidoro in Leon is another UNESCO World Heritage site along the Camino Francés, famous for its Romanesque and Gothic architecture, as well as its stunning frescoes and medieval tombs. Pilgrims can admire the basilica's intricate sculptures and decorative motifs, which offer insights into the religious and artistic traditions of medieval Spain.

Architectural Marvels

Romanesque Churches: Throughout the Camino, pilgrims encounter a wealth of Romanesque churches, chapels, and monasteries that reflect the architectural style of the Middle Ages. These architectural marvels feature ornate carvings, elaborate frescoes, and stunning stained glass windows that showcase the craftsmanship and artistry of the period.

Gothic Cathedrals: Gothic cathedrals, such as the Cathedral of Burgos and the Cathedral of Leon, are prominent landmarks along the Camino Francés, towering over the landscape with their soaring spires and intricate facades.

Pilgrims can marvel at the cathedrals' stunning architecture and decorative details, which serve as testaments to the devotion and skill of medieval craftsmen.

Cultural Events and Festivals

Semana Santa: Holy Week, or Semana Santa, is a major cultural event celebrated throughout Spain, including many towns and cities along the Camino. Pilgrims can witness elaborate processions, religious ceremonies, and traditional rituals that commemorate the passion, death, and resurrection of Jesus Christ, immersing themselves in the rich religious heritage of Spain.

Fiesta de San Fermin: The Fiesta de San Fermin, also known as the Running of the Bulls, is a world-famous festival held in Pamplona, which lies along the Camino Francés. Pilgrims can experience the excitement and spectacle of the festival, watching the running of the bulls and participating in the lively street celebrations that accompany the event.

Culinary Delights

Regional Cuisine: Along the Camino, pilgrims have the opportunity to sample a diverse array of regional cuisines, each reflecting the culinary traditions of the different regions through which they pass. From hearty stews and savory tapas to fresh seafood and artisanal cheeses, pilgrims can savor the flavors of Spain and indulge in the gastronomic delights of the Camino.

Local Markets: Pilgrims can explore local markets and food stalls along the Camino, discovering fresh produce, homemade delicacies, and traditional specialties that showcase the bounty of the land. Whether it's sampling freshly baked bread, tasting local wines, or indulging in sweet pastries, pilgrims can enjoy a culinary journey that delights the senses and nourishes the soul.

Art and Culture

Museums and Galleries: Throughout the Camino, pilgrims encounter a wealth of museums, galleries, and cultural institutions that showcase the art, history, and heritage of the regions they pass through. From contemporary art exhibitions to archaeological treasures, pilgrims can immerse themselves in the cultural riches of Spain and gain a deeper appreciation for its artistic heritage.

Local Traditions: Pilgrims can also experience the vibrant traditions and customs of the regions along the Camino, from traditional music and dance performances to local festivals and celebrations. Whether it's witnessing a flamenco performance in Andalusia or participating in a traditional folk dance in Galicia, pilgrims can engage with the living culture of Spain and forge connections with the people they meet along the way.

How Cultural Highlights Benefit Pilgrims

Enrichment of the Pilgrimage Experience: Cultural highlights along the Camino enrich the pilgrimage experience, offering pilgrims opportunities for learning, exploration, and personal growth. By immersing themselves in the history, art, and culture of the regions they pass through, pilgrims gain a deeper understanding of the significance of the Camino and its place in Spanish heritage.

Connection to the Past: Cultural highlights along the Camino connect pilgrims to the rich tapestry of history and tradition that has shaped the landscape of Spain for centuries. By visiting historic sites, attending cultural events, and sampling regional cuisine, pilgrims engage with the living legacy of the Camino and forge connections to the pilgrims who have walked these same paths before them.

Spiritual Reflection and Contemplation: Cultural highlights along the Camino provide pilgrims with opportunities for spiritual reflection and contemplation, enabling them to connect with the sacred dimensions of the pilgrimage journey. Whether it's visiting a medieval cathedral, attending a pilgrim's mass, or witnessing a religious festival, pilgrims can deepen their faith and find inspiration in the cultural riches of the Camino.

Unveiling the Stories and Legends of the Camino de Santiago: A Comprehensive Exploration

In our quest to provide travelers with a deeper understanding of the Camino de Santiago, we delve into the captivating stories and legends that have shaped this ancient pilgrimage route for centuries. These tales not only enrich the journey but also offer insights into the cultural heritage, spiritual significance, and historical context of the Camino. Here, we offer a more detailed exploration of the stories and legends mentioned earlier, providing readers with a comprehensive guide to the mythical and mystical aspects of their pilgrimage experience.

The Legend of the Cockle Shell

Symbolism and Tradition: Beyond being a mere souvenir, the scallop shell holds profound symbolism for pilgrims on the Camino. Legend has it that the shell represents the various routes pilgrims take to reach Santiago de Compostela, with all paths converging at the final destination. Pilgrims wear the shell as a badge of honor and recognition, signifying their commitment to the journey and their connection to fellow pilgrims.

The Miracle of the Milky Way

Historical Context: The Miracle of the Milky Way, which recounts St. James' miraculous intervention in the Battle of Clavijo, is a foundational legend of the Camino. While historians debate the historical accuracy of the event, the legend underscores the spiritual significance of St. James as the patron saint of Spain and the protector of pilgrims. Pilgrims can reflect on the symbolism of the Milky Way as a guiding light on their pilgrimage journey, leading them toward spiritual enlightenment and divine intervention.

The Story of the Holy Grail

Sacred Relic and Symbolism: The Abbey of San Juan de la Peña, with its association with the Holy Grail, offers pilgrims a glimpse into the realm of medieval legend and religious mysticism. While the authenticity of the Holy Grail remains a subject of debate, the legend serves as a testament to the enduring allure of sacred relics and the power of faith to inspire awe and wonder. Pilgrims can contemplate the symbolism of the Holy Grail as a symbol of spiritual nourishment and divine grace on their pilgrimage journey.

Legends of the Templars

Myth and Mystery: The Knights Templar, with their enigmatic history and legendary exploits, continue to captivate the imagination of pilgrims on the Camino. Stories of hidden treasures, secret rituals, and noble deeds abound, adding an air of intrigue and mystique to the pilgrimage experience. Pilgrims can explore the legacy of the Templars through the medieval churches, castles, and fortresses they encounter along the Camino, pondering the significance of chivalry, honor, and sacrifice in their own spiritual journey.

Folklore of the Galician Countryside

Enchantment and Enigma: The lush landscapes of Galicia, with their verdant forests, misty mountains, and winding rivers, are steeped in folklore and mythology. Pilgrims can immerse themselves in tales of fairies, spirits, and mythical creatures that inhabit the wilds of Galicia, experiencing a sense of wonder and enchantment as they traverse the mystical landscape. These stories serve as reminders of the interconnectedness of nature, spirituality, and the human imagination, inviting pilgrims to embrace the magic of the Camino.

Chapter 7: After the Camino

After completing the Camino de Santiago, pilgrims often experience a profound sense of accomplishment and transformation, but the journey does not end at the steps of the cathedral in Santiago de Compostela. Instead, it marks the beginning of a new chapter filled with reflection, integration, and continued growth. For many pilgrims, the lessons learned and insights gained on the Camino inspire them to carry the spirit of the journey into their daily lives, fostering a deeper sense of gratitude, compassion, and connection with others. Whether returning home or embarking on further travels, pilgrims are forever changed by their pilgrimage experience, carrying the memories and lessons of the Camino with them as they continue their journey of self-discovery and spiritual exploration.

Reflections on Completing the Pilgrimage: A Journey of Self-Discovery and Spiritual Renewal

Completing the Camino de Santiago is a milestone moment for pilgrims, marking the culmination of a physical, emotional, and spiritual journey that extends far beyond the miles walked. As pilgrims stand before the majestic Cathedral of Santiago de Compostela, they are filled with a myriad of emotions – joy, gratitude, awe, and perhaps a hint of sadness at the journey's end. In this reflective piece, we explore the profound impact of completing the pilgrimage, offering insights into the transformative power of the Camino experience and the lessons learned along the Way.

Sense of Accomplishment

Personal Triumph: For many pilgrims, completing the Camino represents a significant personal triumph – a testament to their resilience, determination, and endurance. As they reflect on the challenges overcome, the blisters endured, and the obstacles faced along the Way, pilgrims gain a newfound sense of confidence and self-belief that extends far beyond the physical realm.

Spiritual Renewal

Deepening of Faith: The Camino de Santiago is, at its core, a spiritual journey – a pilgrimage of the soul that invites pilgrims to explore the depths of their faith and spirituality. Upon completing the pilgrimage, many pilgrims experience a profound sense of spiritual renewal, feeling a closer connection to the divine and a deeper understanding of their place in the universe.

Gratitude and Appreciation

Appreciation for Simple Pleasures: The Camino has a way of stripping away the distractions of everyday life, allowing pilgrims to fully appreciate the simple pleasures of existence – a warm meal, a hot shower, a friendly conversation. Upon completing the pilgrimage, pilgrims carry with them a newfound sense of gratitude for life's blessings, both big and small.

Sense of Community

Bonds of Friendship: Along the Camino, pilgrims form deep and lasting bonds with fellow travelers from around the world, united by a common purpose and shared experience. As they reflect on their journey, pilgrims cherish the friendships forged along the Way, recognizing the power of human connection to uplift, inspire, and sustain them through life's challenges.

Lessons Learned

Self-Discovery: Completing the Camino is as much a journey of self-discovery as it is a physical trek across Spain. Along the Way, pilgrims confront their fears, push beyond their limits, and discover hidden reserves of strength and resilience within themselves. As they reflect on their journey, pilgrims gain valuable insights into their own character, values, and priorities, paving the way for personal growth and transformation.

Integration and Continuation

Integration into Daily Life: While the Camino may end in Santiago de Compostela, its lessons and insights continue to resonate long after the journey is over. Pilgrims carry the spirit of the Camino with them as they return to their daily lives, integrating the values of simplicity, compassion, and mindfulness into their interactions and decisions.

Bringing the Camino Spirit Home: Cultivating Mindfulness, Gratitude, and Community in Everyday Life

Completing the Camino de Santiago is not just about reaching Santiago de Compostela; it's about carrying the spirit of the journey with you wherever you go. As pilgrims return home after their pilgrimage, they are faced with the challenge of integrating the lessons learned and insights gained on the Camino into their daily lives. In this detailed exploration, we delve into practical ways to bring the Camino spirit home, fostering mindfulness, gratitude, and community in everyday life.

Cultivating Mindfulness

Daily Practices: Pilgrims can integrate mindfulness into their daily routines by incorporating simple practices such as meditation, deep breathing exercises, or mindful walking. By bringing awareness to the present moment and observing their thoughts and emotions without judgment, pilgrims can cultivate a sense of inner peace and clarity that mirrors the serenity experienced on the Camino.

Connection with Nature: Spending time outdoors and connecting with nature can also foster mindfulness and presence. Pilgrims can seek out green spaces, parks, or natural trails in their local area, immersing themselves in the beauty and tranquility of the natural world.

Practicing Gratitude

Gratitude Journal: Keeping a gratitude journal allows pilgrims to reflect on the blessings and abundance in their lives, no matter how small. Each day, pilgrims can write down three things they are grateful for, whether it's a kind gesture from a friend, a beautiful sunset, or a warm cup of tea. By focusing on the positive aspects of life, pilgrims cultivate a mindset of abundance and appreciation.

Acts of Kindness: Acts of kindness and generosity towards others can also cultivate gratitude and connection. Pilgrims can seek out opportunities to volunteer, donate to charity, or perform random acts of kindness in their community, spreading joy and making a positive impact on the lives of others.

Building Community

Connecting with Fellow Pilgrims: Pilgrims can stay connected with fellow pilgrims they met on the Camino through social media, online forums, or local Camino associations. By sharing their experiences, insights, and challenges with others who understand the journey, pilgrims can maintain a sense of camaraderie and support.

Creating Local Camino Groups: Pilgrims can also create or join local Camino groups or meetups in their area, providing opportunities to share stories, plan future pilgrimages, and participate in Camino-themed events and activities. These local communities serve as a source of inspiration, friendship, and encouragement, keeping the spirit of the Camino alive in their everyday lives.

Living the Camino Values

Simplicity and Minimalism: Pilgrims can embrace the values of simplicity and minimalism by decluttering their homes, simplifying their possessions, and prioritizing experiences over material possessions. By letting go of excess and focusing on what truly matters, pilgrims create space for clarity, freedom, and fulfillment in their lives.

Compassion and Empathy: Practicing compassion and empathy towards oneself and others is another way to embody the spirit of the Camino. Pilgrims can cultivate kindness, understanding, and forgiveness in their interactions, fostering deeper connections and healing relationships.

Continuing Your Journey: Embracing Future Pilgrimages and Utilizing Camino Resources

Completing the Camino de Santiago is often just the beginning of a lifelong journey of self-discovery, exploration, and spiritual growth. As pilgrims return home, they may find themselves longing to embark on future pilgrimages and continue their quest for meaning and connection. In this detailed exploration, we delve into the possibilities for future pilgrimages and the wealth of resources available to support pilgrims on their ongoing journey.

Planning Future Pilgrimages

Exploring Different Routes: While the Camino Francés is the most well-known route, there are numerous other Camino routes to explore, each offering its own unique challenges, landscapes, and cultural experiences. Pilgrims can research and plan future pilgrimages along routes such as the Camino del Norte, Camino Portugués, Camino Primitivo, or Via de la Plata, allowing them to continue their journey of discovery and adventure.

Setting Personal Goals: Pilgrims can set personal goals for future pilgrimages, whether it's completing a specific route, walking a certain number of kilometers, or exploring a particular region of Spain. By setting clear intentions and objectives, pilgrims can stay motivated and focused on their pilgrimage journey, drawing inspiration from the challenges and triumphs of their previous Camino experience.

Utilizing Camino Resources

Guidebooks and Maps: A wealth of guidebooks, maps, and online resources are available to help pilgrims plan and navigate their Camino journeys. Pilgrims can consult guidebooks such as the "Camino de Santiago: The Pilgrim's Guide" or the "Brierley Guide" for detailed route descriptions, accommodation listings, and practical advice. Online forums and Camino websites provide valuable insights and tips from fellow pilgrims, allowing pilgrims to stay informed and connected throughout their journey.

Pilgrim Associations: Pilgrim associations, such as the American Pilgrims on the Camino or the Confraternity of Saint James, offer support, information, and resources to pilgrims embarking on the Camino. Pilgrims can join local chapters, attend events and workshops, and connect with other pilgrims to share experiences and learn from one another.

Deepening Spiritual Practice

Reflective Practices: Pilgrims can deepen their spiritual practice by incorporating reflective practices into their daily lives, such as journaling, meditation, prayer, or contemplative walks. These practices allow pilgrims to integrate the insights and lessons gained on the Camino into their spiritual journey, fostering inner peace, clarity, and connection.

Engagement with Community: Engaging with local spiritual communities, attending religious services, or participating in retreats and workshops can also support pilgrims in their ongoing spiritual growth and exploration. By connecting with others who share similar values and beliefs, pilgrims can find support, inspiration, and camaraderie on their journey.

Living the Camino Values

Service and Giving Back: Pilgrims can embody the values of service and giving back by volunteering, supporting Camino-related initiatives, or participating in pilgrimage-related events and activities. By giving back to the Camino community, pilgrims contribute to the preservation and promotion of this sacred tradition, ensuring that future generations can continue to experience its transformative power.

Living with Intention: Pilgrims can continue to live with intention and purpose, applying the lessons of simplicity, gratitude, and compassion learned on the Camino to their everyday lives. By embracing these values and principles, pilgrims can create a life that is aligned with their deepest values and aspirations, fostering a sense of fulfillment, meaning, and connection.

Appendice
Useful Resources and Websites for Pilgrims on the Camino de Santiago

Embarking on the Camino de Santiago is an exciting and transformative journey, and having access to reliable resources and information can greatly enhance the pilgrimage experience. Whether you're planning your first Camino or embarking on a return journey, here are some invaluable resources and websites to assist you every step of the way:

The Confraternity of Saint James (CSJ)

Website: https://www.csj.org.uk/
Description: The CSJ is a UK-based organization dedicated to promoting the pilgrimage to Santiago de Compostela. Their website offers a wealth of resources, including route guides, accommodation listings, practical advice, and information on pilgrim credentials (Credenciales).

American Pilgrims on the Camino (APOC)

Website: https://americanpilgrims.org/
Description: APOC is a non-profit organization based in the United States that provides support and resources for American pilgrims on the Camino de Santiago. Their website offers practical information, forums, local chapter listings, and resources for planning and preparing for the Camino.

Camino Forums

Website: https://www.caminodesantiago.me/community/
Description: Camino Forums is a popular online community where pilgrims from around the world come together to share their experiences, ask questions, and offer advice. The forums cover a wide range of topics, including route planning, gear recommendations, and personal reflections on the pilgrimage journey.

CaminoGuide.net

Website: https://www.caminoguide.net/
Description: CaminoGuide.net offers comprehensive guidebooks and resources for pilgrims planning their Camino journey. Their website features route descriptions, accommodation listings, packing tips, and practical advice to help pilgrims prepare for the pilgrimage.

Camino de Santiago Official Website

Website: https://www.caminodesantiago.gal/en/
Description: The official website of the Camino de Santiago provides information on the various Camino routes, cultural heritage sites, and practical information for pilgrims. It also offers interactive maps, pilgrimage statistics, and news updates related to the Camino.

Pilgrim Credential (Credencial)

Description: Pilgrims are required to obtain a Pilgrim Credential (Credencial) before starting their Camino journey.

This document serves as a passport for pilgrims, allowing them to stay in pilgrim accommodations (albergues) along the route and collect stamps (sellos) as proof of their journey. Pilgrim Credentials can be obtained from local Camino associations, churches, or online through various pilgrim organizations.

Camino Apps

Description: There are several mobile apps available for pilgrims to use while on the Camino, offering route maps, accommodation listings, and other useful features. Popular apps include WisePilgrim, Buen Camino, and CaminoTool, which provide real-time information and navigation assistance to pilgrims along the route.

Local Tourist Offices

Description: Local tourist offices along the Camino route can provide valuable information and assistance to pilgrims, including maps, route advice, and recommendations for accommodations and attractions. Pilgrims can stop by tourist offices in major cities and towns along the route for personalized assistance and support.

Camino Packing Checklist: Essential Items for Your Pilgrimage

Preparing for the Camino de Santiago requires careful consideration of what to pack to ensure you have everything you need for your journey. This detailed packing checklist covers essential items to bring along on your pilgrimage, helping you stay comfortable, safe, and prepared for the adventure ahead.

Clothing

Lightweight, moisture-wicking shirts
Quick-drying pants or shorts
Breathable underwear and socks (preferably moisture-wicking)
Long-sleeve shirts and pants for cooler weather
Waterproof jacket or poncho
Warm layers (fleece or lightweight down jacket)
Sun hat or cap
Bandana or buff for sun protection
Comfortable walking shoes or hiking boots with good support
Sandals or flip-flops for rest and recovery
Swimwear (for coastal routes or hot weather)

Gear and Equipment

Backpack (30-40 liters) with padded straps and waist belt
Lightweight, compact sleeping bag (preferably rated for cool temperatures)

Travel towel or microfiber towel
Headlamp or flashlight with extra batteries
Trekking poles for stability and support
Water bottles or hydration reservoir
Multi-tool or pocket knife
Duct tape or repair kit
Ziplock bags or dry bags for organization and waterproofing
Travel-size toiletries (soap, shampoo, toothpaste, etc.)
Quick-drying travel towel
Sunglasses with UV protection
Sunscreen and lip balm with SPF
Insect repellent
Personal first aid kit with blister treatment, pain relievers, antiseptic wipes, etc.
Prescription medications and any necessary medical supplies
Personal identification, passport, and pilgrim credential
Cash, credit/debit cards, and emergency contact information

Lightweight travel guidebook or maps
Optional Items

Camera or smartphone for capturing memories
Journal or notebook and pen for recording your thoughts and experiences
Portable charger or power bank for electronic devices
Travel pillow or inflatable pillow for added comfort
Earplugs or noise-canceling headphones for restful sleep
Travel-size laundry detergent for washing clothes along the way
Portable water filter or purification tablets for accessing safe drinking water

Lightweight daypack for exploring towns or carrying essentials during rest days

Tips

Pack light: Aim to keep your backpack weight around 10% of your body weight to avoid strain and fatigue.

Choose moisture-wicking and quick-drying clothing to stay comfortable and prevent chafing.

Test your gear and equipment before your journey to ensure everything works properly and fits comfortably.

Consider the weather and terrain of your chosen Camino route when packing clothing and gear.

Prioritize essential items and leave non-essential luxuries at home to minimize weight and bulk.

Pack items in waterproof bags or liners to protect them from rain and moisture.

Take breaks to adjust your pack weight and redistribute weight as needed for comfort.

Be prepared to adjust your packing list based on your individual needs, preferences, and the specific requirements of your Camino journey.

Sample Itineraries for Different Camino Routes

Embarking on the Camino de Santiago offers pilgrims the opportunity to explore diverse landscapes, historical landmarks, and cultural treasures along various routes. Whether you're seeking a challenging trek through rugged mountains or a leisurely stroll along coastal paths, these sample itineraries provide a glimpse into the unique experiences awaiting pilgrims on different Camino routes.

Camino Francés

Sample Itinerary: 30-Day Journey

Day 1-3: Saint-Jean-Pied-de-Port to Roncesvalles (27 km)
Day 4-6: Roncesvalles to Zubiri (21 km)
Day 7-9: Zubiri to Pamplona (21 km)
Day 10-12: Pamplona to Estella (22 km)
Day 13-15: Estella to Los Arcos (21 km)
Day 16-18: Los Arcos to Logroño (27 km)
Day 19-21: Logroño to Nájera (29 km)
Day 22-24: Nájera to Santo Domingo de la Calzada (21 km)
Day 25-27: Santo Domingo de la Calzada to Belorado (23 km)
Day 28-30: Belorado to Burgos (23 km)

Notes: This itinerary covers the first segment of the Camino Francés, starting from the popular pilgrimage town of Saint-Jean-Pied-de-Port and ending in the historic city of Burgos. It includes a mix of challenging mountain terrain, picturesque villages, and cultural landmarks such as Pamplona and Logroño.

Camino del Norte

Sample Itinerary: 30-Day Journey

Day 1-3: Irun to San Sebastián (25 km)
Day 4-6: San Sebastián to Zarautz (21 km)
Day 7-9: Zarautz to Deba (22 km)
Day 10-12: Deba to Markina-Xemein (21 km)
Day 13-15: Markina-Xemein to Gernika (26 km)
Day 16-18: Gernika to Bilbao (29 km)
Day 19-21: Bilbao to Portugalete (18 km)
Day 22-24: Portugalete to Castro Urdiales (29 km)
Day 25-27: Castro Urdiales to Laredo (27 km)
Day 28-30: Laredo to Güemes (23 km)
Notes: This itinerary follows the northern coast of Spain, offering stunning views of the Cantabrian Sea and picturesque coastal towns. Highlights include the vibrant city of San Sebastián, the cultural hub of Bilbao, and the tranquil countryside of Cantabria.

Camino Portugués

Sample Itinerary: 14-Day Journey

Day 1-3: Lisbon to Santarém (39 km)
Day 4-6: Santarém to Tomar (52 km)
Day 7-9: Tomar to Coimbra (66 km)
Day 10-12: Coimbra to Porto (122 km)
Day 13-14: Porto to Santiago de Compostela (238 km)

Notes: This itinerary begins in the vibrant city of Lisbon and follows the Camino Português Central route through historic towns, lush countryside, and vineyard-covered hillsides. Pilgrims will pass through Coimbra, Portugal's medieval capital, before crossing into Spain and joining the Camino Português Coastal route to Santiago de Compostela.

Camino Primitivo

Sample Itinerary: 18-Day Journey

Day 1-3: Oviedo to Grado (30 km)
Day 4-6: Grado to Salas (30 km)
Day 7-9: Salas to Tineo (31 km)
Day 10-12: Tineo to Pola de Allande (30 km)
Day 13-15: Pola de Allande to Grandas de Salime (31 km)
Day 16-18: Grandas de Salime to Santiago de Compostela (135 km)
Notes: The Camino Primitivo, known as the Original Way, offers pilgrims a challenging and remote journey through the rugged landscapes of Asturias and Galicia. This itinerary covers the final stretch of the route, beginning in the historic city of Oviedo and culminating in Santiago de Compostela, where pilgrims join the Camino Francés to complete their pilgrimage.

Camino Inglés

Sample Itinerary: 5-Day Journey

Day 1: Ferrol to Neda (14 km)

Day 2: Neda to Pontedeume (22 km)
Day 3: Pontedeume to Betanzos (20 km)
Day 4: Betanzos to Bruma (28 km)
Day 5: Bruma to Santiago de Compostela (21 km)
Notes: The Camino Inglés, or English Way, was historically traveled by pilgrims arriving by boat from England and northern Europe. This shorter itinerary begins in the port city of Ferrol and follows a scenic route through coastal villages and lush countryside before arriving in Santiago de Compostela.

Maps
Use Device device to scan QR code for maps

Printed in Great Britain
by Amazon